"Reading G-vites is a wonderful spiritual experience for it reveals to us the many encounters we have with the Divine in our daily lives. This extraordinary book opens our eyes, our minds, and our hearts to make us aware of God being in our lives every day, every moment, but also teaches us how to incorporate God's presence and teachings into our very being."
— Nick Bunick, author of the New York Times bestseller The Messengers

"Once in a while you meet someone who lights up a room when they enter. Even though there is light that vibrates through each of us, when we meet a person who shows us how to love ourselves, we are illuminated in a way that is healing. Patty is the beacon that ignites the spark in all of us."
— Linda McCarthy, a spiritual healer with a Ph.D. in metaphysical counseling, author, and board certified life strategies and holistic health expert

"Patty's book G-Vites made me think of all of the ways God is working in my life, and all of the things I could be doing to recognize those God moments and use them to make my life happier, more spiritual, and less stressful. The way Patty shares struggles from her own life helps to show that we all have times where we feel guilt, frustration, and worry. Her simple techniques to help combat these feelings are remarkably easy to work on, and I'm looking forward to employing them in my own life. G-Vites has already made my life better."
— Lisa Coleman, literary critic and advisor

G-vites
EVERYDAY INVITATIONS FROM GOD

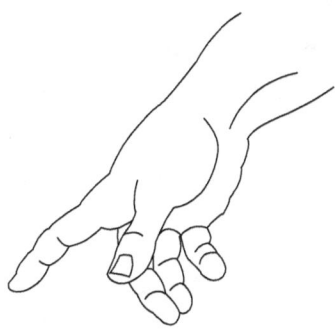

By Patty Ptak Kogutek, Ed.D.

SPIRITUALLY SPEAKING, LLC

Copyright ©2016 Patty Ptak Kogutek

All rights reserved. No part of this book may be used or reproduced by any means, graphic, electronic, or mechanical, including photocopying, recording, tapping or by any information storage retrieval system without the written permission of the publisher except in the case of brief quotations embodied in critical reviews.

Books may be ordered through booksellers or by contacting:
Patty Kogutek
www.pattykogutek.com
1-(406) 885-2225

Because of the dynamic nature of the Internet, any web addresses or links contained in this book may have changed since publication and may no longer be valid. The views expressed in this work are solely those of the author.

The author of this book does not dispense medical advice or prescribe the use of any technique as a form or treatment for physical, emotional, or medical problems without the advice of a physician, either directly or indirectly. The intent of the author is only to offer information of a general nature to help you in your quest for emotional and spiritual well-being. In the event you use any of the information in this book for yourself, which is your constitutional right, the author and publisher assure no responsibility for your actions.

Printed in the United States of America

ISBN: 978-0-9968681-3-6
ISBN: 978-0-9968681-2-9 (e)

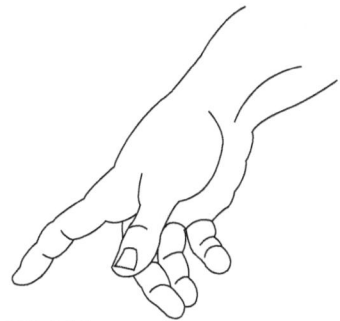

DEDICATION

To my beloved friend, teacher, and husband, Joe, who has taught me the meaning of love, forgiveness, and grace. With gratitude for the many lessons learned at your side on our journey together.

TABLE OF CONTENTS

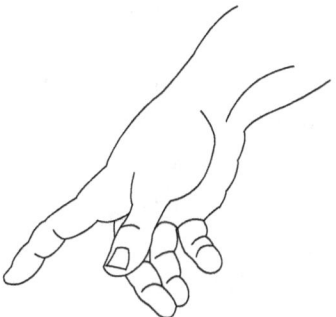

Introduction	xi

Part I: Recognizing G-vites to Fulfill Your Destiny	1

Finding Your Why
- Chapter 1 – Facing the Truth 2
- Chapter 2 – Connecting to the Divine 10
- Chapter 3 – Finding Destiny Through Wisdom 17

Boosting Spiritual Development
- Chapter 4 – Accepting Ourselves 25
- Chapter 5 – Trusting God 32
- Chapter 6 – Gaining Discernment 39

Guarding Your Self-Love
- Chapter 7 – Embracing Failures 46
- Chapter 8 – Summoning Bravery 53
- Chapter 9 – Building Compassion 60

Part II: Trusting G-vites to Survive Adversity 67

Moving on Through Hardships
- Chapter 10 – Developing Honesty 68
- Chapter 11 – Increasing Perseverance 75
- Chapter 12 – Creating Hope 83

Putting Fear and Failure in Their Place
- Chapter 13 – Generating Resilience — 91
- Chapter 14 – Calling Forth Forgiveness — 98
- Chapter 15 – Promoting Confidence — 105

Ditching the Burden of Guilt
- Chapter 16 – Strengthening Courage — 112
- Chapter 17 – Maintaining Sanity — 119
- Chapter 18 – Sustaining Balance — 126

Part III: Celebrating G-vites to Find Happiness — 133

Living in Gratitude
- Chapter 19 – Attuning to Mindfulness — 134
- Chapter 20 – Producing More Patience Through Gratitude — 141
- Chapter 21 – Anticipating Miracles — 149

Creating Abundance
- Chapter 22 – Forging Ahead With Faith — 156
- Chapter 23 – Living in Abundance — 164
- Chapter 24 – Maintaining Wonder — 171

Cultivating Happiness
- Chapter 25 – Gaining Freedom Through Release — 178
- Chapter 26 – Laughing Toward Optimism — 186
- Chapter 27 – Chasing Joy — 193

Note from Patty — 200
Acknowledgments — 201
About the Author — 203

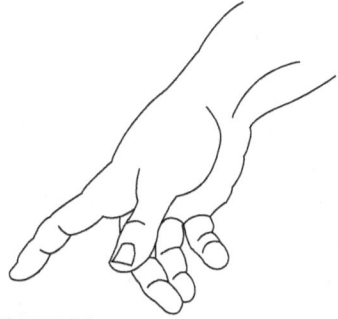

INTRODUCTION

"Is God everywhere?" quizzed a little boy during breakfast with his mother.

"Yes, everywhere," replied his mom.

"Is God here with us in this room?"

"Of course. He is in our kitchen."

"Is God in my cup?"

"Uh…yes." She wondered just where the conversation was leading.

"Gotcha!" The boy slapped both of his hands over the top of the cup. Grinning, he exclaimed, "I caught God."

Like that little boy, we are always searching for God. We are on a lifetime spiritual journey to connect with our Divine Source. We hope to yell, "Gotcha." But so often, our efforts seem to lead to failure rather than success. It's not that God is hiding from us, but that we fail to see the divine invitations extended to us.

God gives us invitations to meet him every day. Every second. God reveals his plan and presence in our lives through G-vites. These G-vites, or invites from God, beckon us to connect with the Divine in a communion.

G-vites are graces offered to us to participate in Divine encounter. We must be ready to recognize them, respond, and learn. G-vites reveal the many facets of God, summoning us to build the relationship and share in the Divine through Love. As humans, we are made for that connection with our Creator.

We can find these G-vites in everyday circumstances. They come as personal invitations; as teachable moments from our Creator to join in the Divine Love expressing itself in virtues. Patience, kindness, humility, stamina to face adversity, and hope are some of the attributes that God extends to us. We can gain these virtues by responding to the G-vite.

For much of my life, I ignored G-vites presented to me in my ordinary day. Instead, I let others define the way to connect with God, seeking the Divine in traditional venues of the church and a convent. In my first book, *A Change of Habit: A Spiritual Journey from Sister Mary Kateri to Sister Mary Vodka*, I shared my spiritual quest. Joining a Catholic convent, I flew onto what I thought was the fast track to God. I ached to yell, "Gotcha," in response to linking to the Divine. I relied on traditional organized religion to lead me to a personal connection with the Divine through prescribed rules, rites, and rituals. The Catholic Church defined my spiritual practices, and I embraced the belief that my relationship with God had to be earned through perfect participation in my religious order.

But the personal connection eluded me. As with the child who caught God in his cup, I thought I had found

God, but I never experienced the Gotcha Moment of Joy. I had to make a tough decision. After seven years of my marriage to Christ, I left the Catholic convent to seek that Gotcha Moment in secular life.

On my own, I floundered. Without my superiors leading the way and overseeing my spiritual development, I felt empty. Disillusionment descended on me. My traditional checklist of religious dogma and customs failed me. I longed to discover how ordinary people, outside a structured religious life, connected with their Creator.

This book is the culmination (so far) of my searching for God. It contains tactics I've used to seek connection with my Creator and how I link with that Divine Love. They are actually skills that lead me to Gotcha Moments. I'm hoping these tactics will work for you, too.

I now know that God is not a divinity to be met on Sundays in church. All the pomp and incense will not draw me closer to God. Nor is God the mean bearded grumpy old man scowling over a ledger of my good and bad actions as depicted in my Catholic prayer books.

Instead, God is an all-loving, everyday God. I've found God in ordinary circumstances, no matter how joyful or sorrowful, calling me into union with the Divine. My life is a gift, and my mission is to be open, receptive, and responding to God's invitations.

So, how do G-vites work?

As each situation in life presents itself, we can respond with one of two choices. We can accept the invitation to change, evolve, and move deeper into the human experience to meet God. Or we can remain in the safety of the status quo defending our own positions, shutting down, or protecting ourselves with shells of non-commitment. What matters is how we RSVP to these vital invitations.

This book will show you how I have found God in ordinary circumstances. You will learn how to listen to your talking soul, calling you to your true life's purpose. You will identify the Divine, dwelling in your everyday life. You will discover how to interpret these lessons to give purpose and meaning to your life. For each lesson, practical steps will help you implement these G-vites.

The book is divided into three main sections: "Recognizing G-vites to Find Your Why," "Trusting G-vites to Find Hope Through Hardship," and "Honoring G-vites to Find Happiness in Celebration."

The first section, "Recognizing G-vites to Find Your Why," introduces steps ensuring your success in identifying G-vites. These chapters include how to identify your destiny, what you need to boost your spiritual development, and how to guard your self-love, all prerequisites to responding to G-vites.

The second section, "Trusting G-vites to Find Hope Through Hardship," shows how to use adversity for transformation, how to let fear and failure fit into our lives, and how to ditch the burden of guilt to live life on your own terms. Adversity invitations are the tougher G-vites to answer.

The final section, "Celebrating G-vites to Find Happiness," speaks to living in gratitude, creating abundance, and helping happiness thrive. These G-vites bring us joy.

The important question is not whether we have found God and whether we can yell "Gotcha." The bigger question is when God sends the G-vites to us in our every day circumstances, are we able to RSVP or do we merely trash the invitation. The choice is ours.

We are made for connection with our Creator. Don't waste another minute holding out for the "Gotcha" and looking for God in all the wrong places.

Here is your personal invitation. Let's learn to RSVP!

PART I

RECOGNIZING G-VITES TO FULFILL YOUR DESTINY

Finding Your Why

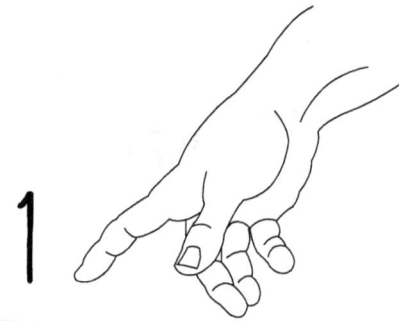

1
FACING THE TRUTH

The truth will set you free, but first it will piss you off.
—Gloria Steinem

I've been compared to looking like Julia Roberts or Carol Channing more times than I can count. The Julia Roberts association flatters me, but Carol Channing? That comparison, probably due to my mouth, makes me cringe.

One morning in a Montana bagel shop, I caught the young girl behind the counter staring at me. Feeling her eyes fixed on my face, I chatted up my friend to distract myself from the uncomfortable situation. As we made our way to a table, I spied the girl's piercing eyes still following me, step by step. They noted my every move, making me feel like a petri dish specimen.

In illogical retaliation, I lathered my sesame seed bagel with a healthy dose of cream cheese. As I thickened the cheese layer, the shop owner approached our table. I twitched from side to side in my seat, feeling an impending reprimand like I had broken a school rule. The owner leaned down as if to convey a secret, but broadcasted her statement far above a whisper: "Allison, behind the counter, wants to know if you are Julia Roberts' mother."

At first I thought I misheard the statement. I paused and looked at the counter girl. Then, the word "Mother" sunk in.

"MOTHER," I repeated louder than I would have liked. Noticing the eavesdropping ears at surrounding tables, I defended my age. "I'm Julia Roberts, NOT her mother." Forcing out a stiff laugh, I threw my shoulders back daring anyone to object despite my white hair.

But the age truth needled me. Shrinking into my seat, I whined at my friend. "Every one in the whole world thinks I'm Julia Roberts' mother. I'm not that old!"

"Yeah, you are, honey," my friend grinned. "We both are."

I pouted. She smirked. Resigning to truth, I had to join her laughter.

FACING THE TRUTH

Happiness lies with the truth, however painful that may be. Facing the truth can be uncomfortable. But that's the place we must start. Confronting the hard cold facts is a good starting point for finding our why, our purpose for being on earth.

Admitting the truth in this case—that I was not indeed Julia Roberts and could in fact be as old as her mother—

forced me to accept my human timeline. I had to accept where I really was to move forward. Granted, this is a silly situation, far from on par with larger truths we face. But the process can apply to larger life issues.

Accepting the truth is one of the hardest obstacles to overcome. Being honest and facing reality is a prerequisite for determining our destiny. If we pay attention, we can discover G-vites that hold our truth. That G-vite in the bagel shop invited me to be honest with my age and learn to laugh at myself.

Someone once told me, "It's not the cruise I signed up for, but it's the ship I'm on." That sums up how to face the truth. No self-delusions, no lies. Honesty is a hallmark of a fully mature individual. Mature individuals don't play the pretend game or lie to themselves or others. An honest person is up front, rather than evasive with words. Opposite from being the Queen or King of Denial, they face reality the way it is rather than using self-delusional behavior to mask it. They do not have to rationalize their thoughts to make themselves successful in their minds. They have no need to distort their own reality to make themselves feel better.

We do not live in Camelot. We are not built for perfection. Everything is not grand, nor is it meant to be. We need to say, "My child may not be the ideal child, and my partner may not be Mr. or Mrs. Perfect, but this is the ship I'm on."

The first step in the journey is total honesty with ourselves. To trek down the road of truth, we must begin with ourselves and radiate truth out to others. We need to be receptive to G-vites that come from inside us or outside us to help us grasp truth.

GOD'S INVITATION: TRUTH

A Japanese legend says that we have three faces. The first face we show to the world, putting our best appearance for all to see. The second face we show to our family and close friends, probably a truer depiction of who we are. The third face is the one we never show anyone. That is the truest reflection of who we really are.

We are so fearful of facing the truth and showing our real selves. We are afraid that we will not be loved or accepted. We are afraid we will be criticized.

So how do we get past those fears to live our truth? How do we get in touch with our inner self to proclaim our truth to the world? The first baby step in this process combines attention to our inner self and what we represent to the world.

Take, for example, this common communication pattern:

"Patty, would you take over the presidency of our school parent association next year?"

"NO," screams my gut, tightening with apprehension. But my mouth flaps, "Yes, I'd be glad to."

This communication demonstrates the small lies we live with daily. Our mouths say one thing but our insides feel the opposite. We do not want to say "no." We do not want to disappoint others. We work hard to get others to love and respect us, so we sacrifice ourselves—our own time, energy, and desires—for the sake of others.

Those gut feelings can be G-vites. They can be invitations from God to listen to our inner selves. They can be invitations to align our feelings with what we do or say to create our truth.

To unite the inner and outer selves, we need to develop Gut Alignment. This gut-check helps us coordinate the words spewing from our mouths with the feelings that our emotions are causing in our physical bodies. That gut feeling has to be in sync with the mouth. Both must function in unison to enjoy the benefits of truth; a steppingstone to finding our why, our purpose, our destiny.

Gut Alignment consists of three parts: speaking what we feel, measuring success, and preparing for reactions to change. Let's look at how to implement these three parts of Gut Alignment.

1. SPEAK WHAT WE FEEL

Initially, in the Gut Alignment, we need to zero in on how we REALLY feel about something rather than how we SHOULD feel. Our bodies give us clues about our emotions: muscle twitches, headaches, upset stomachs, or shortness of breath. We must listen to what our bodies are telling us to discover what we really want. My emotions always cause my stomach to tighten, so I focus on my torso muscles.

Once we discover what we REALLY want, we must summon the courage to share it with others. Finding the words to describe how we actually feel will give others the information that they need to read us. Lengthy explanations of why are unnecessary. A simple "I think I'll have to pass" or "That won't work for me" can do the trick of protecting what we really want while communicating with politeness.

Build up skills in saying "no" to others. Practice saying "no" to smaller things before leaping into saying "no" to bigger things.

2. MEASURE SUCCESS

When we make decisions to please others, we measure our success by their happy reactions. We please people by doing things their way. When we speak what we feel, oftentimes going against what other people want from us, we must engage in a new measure of success. Instead of gauging success by the reactions of others, we must evaluate success based on our own reaction. We must ask ourselves the question: "Did I please myself or others?"

Because we may disappoint someone else, we must learn to care for ourselves with affirmations. Try out self-affirmations, such as "What others think of me is none of my business" or "I realize that others may be disappointed, but I'm protecting my own happiness."

3. PREPARE FOR REACTIONS TO CHANGE

When establishing what we really feel, we may surprise others. Spouses, family, friends, or co-workers may react differently as we break away from our past conciliatory behavior. In the Dance of Life, we move in syncopation with those around us. For instance, as a dance partner, I feel and respond to the steps of others, often following their lead. They move; I respond. I anticipate their movements, and they anticipate mine. We reassure ourselves that we know each other's reactions to the music.

Our dance partners expect to see certain behaviors from us based on our past behaviors. People know how we will react in certain situations. They count on us to behave as they expect. We are predictable.

But what happens when we make changes that are counter to what people expect? Small changes, such as an innovative hairstyle or a new diet, may slide right into the dance like an added toe tap. But more radical changes—a shift in a major point of view or steps to claim more control of our lives—can trip up partners. Larger changes complicate the dance, causing us to step on our partner's toes. By altering deeply entrenched behaviors, we may blindside them to the point where the dance fails to function. Partners may stumble instead into silent treatments, cold shoulders, or shunning.

Adding to the difficulty of the dance, we may not be comfortable with the changes within us. Some changes I've undertaken pushed me far out of my comfort zone until I adapted. We need time to adjust. Likewise, we can expect nothing less from our dance partners as they reel back at us with, "What in the world is going on?"

Our partners may level us with attacks: "People could always count on you. Why do you seem so different?" We must prepare to explain sudden changes and embrace the reactions from those that thought they knew us. We may need to forge ahead without their blessings.

This same dance can occur along the path of our spiritual development. We need to stay firm in our spiritual beliefs, choosing those elements that move us forward. As long as we follow the lead of our hearts with love, we will be in step with our destiny. The dance still goes on, with or without the blessing of those around us. Just remember, we have the choice of how we will dance! We can dance in reaction to everyone around us, or dance to our own truth. God invites us to dance to our inner truths.

PRAYER

Dear Lord, help me to face the truth within myself, knowing that nothing that I can do will ever change your love for me.

2
CONNECTING WITH THE DIVINE

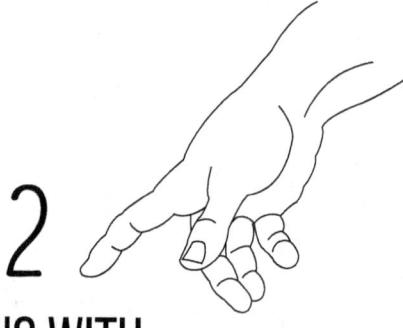

You were put on this earth to achieve your greatest self, to live out your purpose, and to do it courageously.
—Steve Maraboli, Life, the Truth, and Being Free

"Hindsight is 20/20," says the adage. I could have saved myself anguish in tracking down my life's purpose, my why, if I had just looked in the rear view mirror. Leanings revealed themselves at an early age. They just never snagged my attention.

Even as a first grader at St. Margaret Mary's Catholic Elementary School in Omaha, Nebraska, my parents and the nuns expected me to be a good student. That was part of being Catholic. At six years old, I felt the responsibility of high expectations dropped in daily doses of behavioral requirements. During October, our class took on a project to get our families to recite the rosary every day. Every evening, I marked the little box, indicating my family had complied in praying the rosary.

At the end of the month, the school awarded prizes for all the families that had a check in all 31 boxes.

Of course, my checklist had 31 days marked. While some kids blew off the project and others cheated by checking off family devotions just to get the assignment done, I actually cajoled my family to do our devotion every night. As incentive, I led them in it.

During that month, my parents went out for the evening, leaving my two sisters and me at home with our regular neighborhood babysitter Mary. Even though her name sounded Catholic, she was a non-Catholic who attended the local public high school. My father called her drill team attire skimpy, but I spent the evening taking stock of every cool thing she did.

My parents expected us to be dutiful for Mary. My younger sister Peggy and I, usually models of children-are-to-be-seen-and-not-heard, strove to please our parents. When my parents returned, my mother asked for a report of our behavior.

"Yes. They were good." Mary gave my parents the anticipated answer. "But I was just wondering…just how long does it take to say the rosary?"

"Our family says the rosary every night," my father boasted. "It takes us about 15-20 minutes. Why do you ask?"

"When I went to put Patty in bed for the night at 8:30, she said that she had to say the rosary."

"That's understandable. She leads our family in reciting the rosary every night for her class project."

"Well, it took Patty more than an hour to say her rosary. And during it, there seemed to be a lot of noise and laughter upstairs with the girls."

Busted. Non-Catholic Mary had caught on to our misbehavior. That was the last time that I used the rosary as my stay-up-late excuse with Mary. But even with the giggles, I found the spiritual ritual important.

CONNECTING WITH THE DIVINE

Few people know or recognize their life's destiny at age six. Including me. Early on, the signs of a spiritual teacher unfolded, but I had no understanding of what they meant. If I wasn't leading the family in the rosary, I wrapped a towel around my head as a veil. Dressed like a nun, I taught my dolls and sisters, my pretend students. Catholic Digest, a clone of Readers Digest but filled with Catholic stories, even wrote a short piece about my personal devotion to reciting the rosary.

Leading the family in reciting the rosary and dressing up like a nun may have been simply signs of my interpretation of the world around me. But they may have also been the lighter hand of divine guidance. Childhood events such as these could have been G-vites. But I didn't recognize them.

G-vites do not always arrive with horns honking or music blaring. Often, they are subtle. Sometimes recognizing G-vites requires a sacred space, a place where we can take the time to be still, a routine during which we can connect with the divine.

Mother Teresa knew the value of stillness. Her business card read, "In the silence of the heart, God speaks." She knew the busy-ness of our world works to disrupt our spiritual connection. She sought silence to help build that connection. To achieve the stillness Mother Teresa advocated requires discipline.

Convents used stillness as a means to achieve detachment. As a nun, I strove to shun earthly distractions of attachments. My vows as a nun included living in poverty, directly aimed at removing material goods as temptations of the world and opening the door to the heavenly kingdom adorned with spiritual goods. This detachment from the things of this world, practiced through meditation, prayer, and lifestyle, was designed to provide time for connecting with the divine.

But that detachment employed a divisive approach, separating heaven and earth—and therefore splitting the body from the soul. The rhetoric of detachment disparaged the human body and earthly goods that lead to spiritual ruin. That false dichotomy of spiritual versus earthly forced a black and white, either-or choice. Instead, God's material gifts can be used as steppingstones. The temporal and spiritual can complement each other, especially in spiritual routines. We can enjoy the beauty of this world and all its pleasures while still finding a connection with our Creator.

Instead of shunning worldly joys, we must employ detachment in another way in our spiritual rituals. We must separate ourselves from things that hinder connection between the Spirit and us: toxic people spewing negativity, old beliefs flinging out guilt and fear, judgmental attitudes, and material objects becoming obsessions. Removing our attachments to them can create space for a clear connection with God. Only then can we be open for G-vites to come through the stillness.

So where do we start to detach and connect? Just like my leading the family in daily recitation of the rosary, we need to create time for spiritual routines that will allow for connection with God. To carve out time for spiritual routines to improve our ability to hear G-vites, we need to explore ways to combine worldly joys with divine conversation.

GOD'S INVITATION: DETACHMENT AND CONNECTION

Making the divine connection a routine spiritual practice is essential. Just like nourishing relationships with friends and family members, we need to make time to cultivate the spiritual practice of internal communication. This divine connection requires both prayer and meditation for a balanced conversation.

Simply, prayer is talking with God, while mediating is listening to God. No one likes people who monopolize conversations. The same is true with our conversation with God. We can't just pelt God with our requests and needs, we need to listen for answers. Surprisingly, the words "silent" and "listen" use the same letters. Listening requires silence. That strong connection between the two leads us to a spiritual relationship with our Creator and opens us to G-vites.

For meditation and prayer, find what works for you. Carve out a time of day that lends itself to your schedule and pick a form of connection that complements your personality and lifestyle. This communion time can take on many different forms. Let's look at six ways to add meditation to your daily schedule.

- **Traditional meditation:** While many books outline structured methods of meditation, you can make traditional meditation simpler. I start by concentrating on three things: quieting my mind, finding the joy within, and opening myself to guidance from my Source. By limiting my reflections to these three things, the stillness lets me connect with God.

- **Meditative walking:** Many times I cannot sit still for traditional mediation, so I use meditative walking. Choose a natural path outdoors with trees, foliage, meadows, birds, or water. Instead of mulling over things bugging you, hone in on the details of nature. Through appreciation of what you see or hear, you can interpret G-vites.

- **Listening to music:** Music can shape our moods. But rather than letting the tunes lilt in the background as you do things, sit with the sole intention of listening. Do nothing else. Choose music that improves your mood. Don't get boxed in to listening to traditional spiritual music. When 27 musicians came together to sing the Beach Boys hit "God Only Knows," I found meditating on the music led to elation.

- **Guided meditation:** Recordings of guided meditations can direct your thoughts. For some, that direction helps keep the mind from wandering off track. I keep a few guided meditations on my cellphone. In the middle of the night when worry and fear keep me awake, I can quiet my angst by listening to one.

- **Yoga:** Part exercise, part meditation, yoga connects the body and soul through quieting the mind while building flexibility and strength. Yoga means "union," the union of the body, mind, and soul. If you've never done yoga, find a beginning yoga class to explore this meditative practice.

- **Labyrinths:** The ancients use meditative walking to forge a connection with the divine. They followed prescribed routes in mazes to avoid the mental activity of deciding on where to direct steps. In doing so, they freed their minds to be open to another voice. While you don't need a real labyrinth, you can create your own meditative walking route by predetermining your route ahead of time. Suspend all thoughts, while walking, to concentrate on feelings and whims within.

In the beginning, delving into spiritual practice may feel awkward. Start small with fifteen minutes per day. Step away from your normal mental and physical routine. Sit, breathe, relax. Just be. Open up the passageways, and feel the energy of the connecting flow. Remember, there is not one right way, giving you the permission to merely be.

A release of ties that inhibit a spiritual freedom is essential for responding to suggestions from within. Only then can you hear yourself speak. Only then can you hear G-vites. Only then can you find your life's mission.

PRAYER

Dear Lord, let me feel your divine presence. Help me to connect to the sacred awe in this life, leading me to fulfill my life's mission.

3

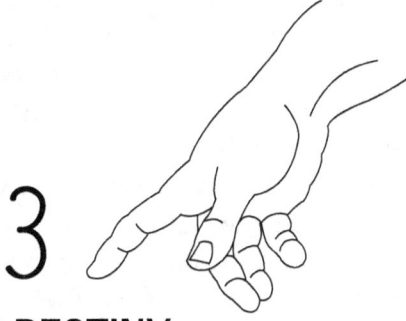

FINDING YOUR DESTINY THROUGH WISDOM

The purpose of life is the lesson. —Shannon L. Alder

"Heaven! There's even a picture of heaven in this book," I exclaimed in wonderment to my husband Joe. With my mouth gaping, in an unladylike fashion, I paged though a book on display in a Barnes and Noble Bookstore. My heartbeat sped up. The afterlife: That's what it looks like. I thumbed through for more pictures of the other side.

While my husband Joe and I dodged Montana snow showers by whiling away an afternoon in the bookstore, I looked through Sylvia Browne's book Life on the Other Side. Its subtitle—A Psychic's Tour of the Afterlife—made my eyes bug out. Good Catholics didn't consult psychics, but I felt riveted to this book.

I've always been a spiritual seeker, searching to make contact with my Creator to shed light on my existence. But my spiritual journey, including seven years spent as a nun, clung to the traditional Catholic route. In the bookstore, Browne's actual pictures of heaven rattled me. I felt the blood drain from my head.

Sure, I had been looking for some interest-grabbing material for cold blustery days. Browne's book was far from what I expected to find and certainly outside the normal Catholic experience. But her book intrigued me. My eyes glued to each image and her words as I paged through the book. Who was this Sylvia Browne woman? How did she know about life beyond the Pearly Gates? And how could she be so brash as to publish several drawings of the rooms of heaven?

Up until this point, Catholicism dominated my reading list. I even sprinkled in less strict Jesuit authors for good measure! But with Browne's book in my hands, I teetered on the edge of my comfort zone, torn between returning the book to the shelf like a good Catholic and desiring to comprehend the psychic's view of heaven.

Despite feeling like I violated Catholic law by even browsing the work, I clung to the book instead of returning it to the shelf. As if my hands knew what my head needed, I fanned the pages back and forth just to be sure no demons jumped out. Then, I marched up to the sales counter and bought it.

Sylvia Browne won me over with that first book. Raised also as a Catholic, she shared a similar upbringing as me, with Catholic schools and stringent rules. I identified with her stories, and she worked from my same faith-based understandings. But where I merely followed the rules of Catholicism, Browne went further, melding her intuitive skills into her practice. She argued her vision of the afterlife articulately with common sense and documentation. No amount of my meager faith could counter her findings.

Browne stressed the importance of knowing your life's

purpose. Yikes! Here I was, in my early fifties, newly retired as an elementary school administrator, and having failed my big spiritual journey in the convent. But still I couldn't answer one simple question: What was I here for?

Without children, my purpose wasn't to raise a beautiful loving family. With my aging parents in Southern California while we lived in Montana, my calling wasn't to help them. With retiring early, my destiny certainly was no longer making an impact on educating the youth of the world. Just what was I here for? Yes, I could throw a great dinner party. But that's hardly a life's purpose.

With one lifetime, we have one chance to get it right. To avoid squandering whatever gifts I might possess, I made an appointment with Sylvia Browne for a reading to find out my life's purpose. Even though my religious upbringing condemned consulting a psychic or an intuitive, I figured God would give me a pass this one time because I was stumped.

For two years, I waited on Sylvia's list to get a chance to ask her my questions. When we talked, she told me that my life's purpose was that of caregiver. I was meant to shoulder responsibility. Sylvia then explained how I could fulfill that role as caregiver, by saying, "One day, you will write a book that will help many people."

I ignored her words. After all, I had nothing to say that would help anyone. In doing so, I turned a deaf ear to my soul's voice.

Eight years later, Sylvia proved to be right. I did publish a book. I discovered that I did have a story to tell and that it was one that could help others. The story of my seven years as a nun and overcoming my Catholic guilt took shape in *A Change of Habit*.

FINDING YOUR "WHY"

Oscar Wilde wrote that the two most important days in your life are the day you were born and the day you realize why. But discovering your why is tough. The biggest deterrent is our own minds.

During a discussion in my Intuitive Development class, the instructor referred to the nonstop rational and irrational thoughts that beseech our minds as listening to the "drunken monkey." This drunken monkey that sounds so harmless can skew our journeys to happiness.

The drunken monkey sits on our shoulders chattering about what we SHOULD do and what we OUGHT to feel. It blathers away, rerunning useless messages about fear, guilt, and what ifs. The noise clutters our ability to listen within and be receptive to G-vites. In our efforts to please others on the outside, we block our authentic selves and the Spirit directing us every day. Spiritual direction comes through our feelings and emotions, the chosen language of the soul. But listening to the monkey disables the messages from within.

This drunken monkey sets us up to feel badly because our feelings conflict with the SHOULDS or OUGHTS. The monkey says, "Good girls don't get angry," so we feel like failures because we indeed feel angry. The monkey says, "A real man wouldn't be sad," or "A mature person wouldn't feel jealous." But we do feel sad or jealous, feelings we must acknowledge to move on.

Because of the conflict between what the monkey says we should do and what we feel inside, we flounder in a quagmire of indecision. We stall. We become deaf to the voice from within. When I discovered Browne's book in the bookstore, the drunken monkey told me that good Catholics don't buy books written by psychics. By purchasing the book, I slapped that monkey down opening myself to God's message. But my chattering doubtful mind worked overtime again, as I waffled for four years before heeding Browne's suggestion to put my journey into a book. I let the drunken monkey manipulate my mind into indecision due to fear of potential failure.

So how do we get out of our drunken monkey minds? How do we get instead into our feeling hearts where we can detect G-vites to find our why? How to we gain the wisdom from within?

GOD'S INVITATION: WISDOM

Wisdom is the virtue of using our experiences to give us common sense and insight into life. We usually think that with age comes wisdom. But not necessarily. Sometimes old age just shows up by itself!

God invites us to do the work it takes to acquire wisdom. Gaining wisdom takes both internal and external practice. It requires being honest with ourselves on the inside and adjusting the wisdom to our external situations.

So how do we gain internal and external wisdom?

Wisdom is the result of learning when we are searching for other things. Learning is dependent upon honest reflection. It's a combination of observing, reflecting, and adapting our outward behaviors. I raced through my life striving to live up to the expectation of others, but seldom took the time needed for personal growth. I discovered that it's never too late to begin this inner search for wisdom.

Integrating wisdom into my external life takes constant practice. One method that has worked for me is reflective journaling.

For some people, keeping a journal comes naturally, like writing in a daily diary. For others, like myself, this self-observation is hard work. It requires me to delve deeper into some of the feelings that I choose for some reason to ignore. It takes time, discipline, and personal questioning to engage in useful journaling.

Reflection is essential in identifying feelings and what they mean in responding to G-vites. Reflection will uncover the cause of your uneasiness, those draining, depressing feelings that are communicating important messages to you. Examining how you contribute to these feelings and from where the pain stems will allow you to see what you can do to change them to move you into closer connection to God—to move you closer to wisdom.

The method that has worked for me in taking stock is a "Destiny Inventory." To create a Destiny Inventory, take a page and divide it into four quadrants. Label the quadrants:

- What is working for me
- What is not working for me
- What happiness would look like
- What I need to do

Once you have your page set up, fill in the quadrants. Let's examine what you should investigate using each of these quadrants.

In the first quadrant, titled "What is working for me," make a list of positive attributes working in your life. List your personal strengths and skills. Identify situations in which you excel. Examine the people around you—friends, family, and co-workers—specifying those who support and nourish you. Only list those who have a positive affect on you.

In the second quadrant, you'll need to dig into what is not working for you. Look at situations that you find uncomfortable, especially those that drain your mental, physical, and psychological energy. Be sure to include in the list any people who may be toxic for you: the constant complainers, the braggarts, the intimidators, the intolerant, and the unaccepting. Identify any negativity in your life.

In the third quadrant, look at what happiness would look like for you. Be specific. List anything that would make your soul sing. Does music enhance your day? Maybe gardening brings you peace. What lights up your life?

In the fourth quadrant, examine what you need to do. Here's where you must create an action plan, what do you need more of, less of and what adjustments must be made to obtain them. The plan needs to address building healthy relationships and pulling back on those that do not feed your soul.

Initially, the reflective journaling may seem cumbersome because it takes time to dig deeply into how you feel. It may also be painful for you to evaluate uncomfortable situations, especially if they have persisted for some time. But being honest with yourself and your situation is the first step in responding to God's invitation. It is the first step toward gaining common sense and insight into your life. It is the first step to acquiring wisdom.

PRAYER

Dear Lord, help me to listen to my soul's yearnings pulling me in your direction. Help me to be true to myself and my life's work in order to gain the wisdom you want me to have.

Boosting Spiritual Development

4 ACCEPTING OURSELVES

Wanting to be someone else is a waste of the person you are. —Marilyn Monroe

The plane cruised at 37,000 feet for the last hour as I tried to read, sleep, and busy myself with no success. Pinned in the dreaded middle seat, I felt trapped by both men on either side of me. Appearing as two stone-silent pillars of salt, they were plugged in to their electronics, hooked up and totally unaware of me.

On my right by the window, my husband, Joe, numbed himself for flights by immersing himself in crossword puzzles, Sudoku, or the New York Times on his iPad. I have learned to live with his silence.

But the aisle man, that silent statuesque man on my left, never even gave me eye contact when I crawled over him to take my center seat. This complete stranger made no attempt to interact. No nod or smile. He obviously wanted his privacy. Understanding that, I intended to honor his wish.

Not wanting to disturb him and his addiction to his phone connection, I twisted into the contortions of a Cirque de Soleil stuntwoman to find a comfortable position. I squirmed to pull my iPad from my bag on the floor—anything to occupy my mind while stuck between two non-conversant travelers. With no Internet access, I opted for Bingo.

Opening the game, I chose to play two cards instead of one to up the challenge. As the number balls dropped down from the Bingo heavens on the screen, I scanned both of my cards for the matching digits and daubed their boxes when found.

Win one, lose two. The games tallied up in the boredom of the flight. Lost in the numbers, I sensed movement on my left. A huge hairy arm reached over into my space with a finger pointing to a number I had missed on one of my cards. Riveting my eyes on the screen, intent not to miss any more numbers, I pressed on.

Then once again, the pointy finger invaded my Bingo territory, highlighting two more numbers I had overlooked, one on each card. That put the pressure on, but because I knew he was watching, I fumbled. I couldn't focus on the game. "He thinks I'm one blithering idiot," I squirmed, knowing I was missing another number.

The silent stone of a man plucked off his headphones and announced, "Ma'am, you should only be playing one card at a time." His glare drove home the point that I was not skilled enough to play two cards at a time.

I had to laugh. At Bingo, despite my Ph.D., I was a blithering idiot.

I relayed the scene to my 92-year-old mother, who wins Bingo in her assisted living home. She rebuked me, "Patty, you have to pay attention!" Her words seemed to carry more import, as if my failure at Bingo summed up my life.

Rolling my eyes, I laughed. At least I could accept my failure at Bingo.

ACCEPTING OURSELVES

I have a favorite saying, "We never quite see ourselves as others see us." The man next to me on the airplane and my mother both saw me as lacking skills for a child's game. How mortifying to be called out for an elementary numbers game with my Ph.D. hanging on the wall!

While the man and my mother may have deemed me inept, inside I recognized that my self-definition did not rely on their judgment on a singular incident. I could accept my lack of Bingo skills knowing that I had other skills.

Eric Barker, writer for the *New York Times*, the *Wall Street Journal*, and *Time*, explained how self-acceptance works in his piece, "How to Stop Feeling Guilty: Five Secrets Backed by Research." He explains that we are not our actions. We may be responsible for them, but they do not define us. He borrows the USA concept from psychologist Albert Ellis in order to make his point. The concept of USA, Universal Self Acceptance, means that we need to accept ourselves for who we are. We may experience remorse about what we did. But we are not bad because of our behavior.

If I follow the philosophy of USA, then I can accept myself for who I am, regardless of whether I play Bingo well or not. I can also accept myself for my positive attributes as well as shortcomings.

Sometimes, in order to accept our limitations, we need to learn humility. I have a divine part of me that calls me to Godly connection, but I shudder when my frailties of human nature show up. The practice of humility honors both the divine and human sides of life.

Learning humility means accepting our humanity. Realizing that we are not the only ones battling disappointments, lacks, and fiascos is a place to start. All of us share financial concerns. We all have personal hardships. Every family experiences pressures. Failures bind us together as humans.

If we change our perspective on our shortcomings, we can ease the burden of carrying them. We don't need to be embarrassed by our failures. Instead, we can adopt humility, by recognizing that we have flaws in common with the rest of humanity. In turn, our comrades in failure can make us feel lighter—knowing we are not alone in dealing with doubts and worry.

To develop the humility to accept ourselves, we must throw out the perfect life façade. Once we give up the need for perfection, we find amazing connections with each other. All humans share similar longings, desires, struggles, and failures.

Things don't always go according to our plans or desires. Sometimes, we aren't the people that we want to be. Instead of acting with divine compassion, we can be unkind, mopey, angry, vulnerable, and insecure. There is nothing wrong with us. Those are human traits. Humility can help us face those with USA, or Universal Self Acceptance.

In order to be happy, we need to accept our situations, accept ourselves, and accept others—failures and all, just as we are. When we open our hearts to accepting ourselves with humility as part of the human race, we see things differently. Instead of striving for perfection, we can relax in humble gratitude that we share a bond with all those around us.

Let's put down the burden of seeking perfection. Instead, let's open up to a wonderful secret: Shhh… WE ARE ALL HUMAN!

GOD'S INVITATION: ACCEPTANCE

What is acceptance? Acceptance is the virtue that enables us to deem the unchangeable circumstances in which we find ourselves as satisfactory. It's not a passive quality of merely sitting there doing nothing. It's an act of assent to the reality of the situation. It's an active conscious choice of approval.

That sounds easy. But it's difficult.

How do I get the virtue of acceptance? To begin with, we must shift our mindset. We need to understand that we do not have the control button. We must loosen our grip on the circumstances of life and give way to the flow of life. We must believe and live in internal harmony, even if things are falling apart externally. As Mom used to say, "Everything works out for the best." We have to believe that. With this deep belief in the synchronicity of our lives, trusting that everything that happens is part of the bigger picture in God's plan for us, we can relax. We can achieve that "peaceful easy feeling."

How can you practice going with the flow and integrate the virtue of acceptance? To develop this powerful attitude, we must raise our awareness to knowing that everything is in perfect order.

Creating a flow chart to describe the connections and influences can help. A flow chart can visually depict the sequential steps in the process of your life.

- **Step 1:** Begin by drawing boxes in a horizontal line filling them with major, life altering occurrences. These boxes will depict the meaningful experiences in your life.

- **Step 2:** Draw the connecting arrows showing how one incident leads to the next. These connections demonstrate the dependency of the flow of life.

- **Step 3:** See the pivotal points and how they hinge on one another. They line you up to where you are today.

I recently saw "The Making of 'Gone With the Wind'" exhibit at the Harry Ransom Center at the University of Texas at Austin. The storyboard for the "Burning of Atlanta" scene reinforced just how helpful it would be to see our lives as a movie story. Movie storyboards are the ultimate flow chart. Touring that exhibit, I saw that although we are not the producers of our lives, we certainly are the directors. We control the choice of our attitude and how we react as our lives unfold in a single story.

In movie format, my life scenes would show divorce with zooming in on forgiveness, the death of a friend resolving into love and appreciation, and holiday celebrations for treasured family times together. Seeing our life stories segmented into frames can help us see the Divine Order that may be at work.

For me, a flow chart has helped reinterpret prior events in my life. I could dismiss my seven years in the convent as wasted time, or see those years as giving me the experience of suffering guilt. In the bigger picture of my life, those years are important as they set me up to help others struggling with guilt.

In your flow chart, look for silver linings. See the good in everything and everyone. Observe the harmony of events, remaining in a conscious state of acceptance. Only seeing the positive may not be rational or logical, but remember this is a lesson of acceptance for your unseen, irrational, and illogical soul.

Trace the synchronicity. Put on your hindsight glasses to discover how things have all come together for the best in the past. You might have thought that things couldn't have been worse, but somehow you managed to get through them. That means you are batting 1,000. Keep that uplifting attitude.

PRAYER

Dear Lord, I know you are the perfect creator designing the perfect harmony ending with our highest good. Please grant me the acceptance that I need to go with your Universal Flow knowing that it will all come together in the end for the BEST.

5

TRUSTING GOD

We must cease striving and trust God to provide what He thinks is best and in whatever time He chooses to make it available. But this kind of trusting doesn't come naturally. It's a spiritual crisis of the will in which we must choose to exercise faith.
—Charles R. Swindoll

"Dear Lord, I'm getting impatient! You, above all others, should know our house has been on the market for too long without so much as one offer. You know how much time, energy, and money we have put into this project. It's time for it to sell."

I begged God for help in selling our house in Montana. Over the past several years, our home in Arizona had transitioned into our main residence. The Montana house weighed on us like excess baggage.

We had updated our northern home with heated travertine floors, huge flat screen TVs, and even an original ski lift chair in our front yard. But between the lagging real estate market and my anxiousness to quit the seasonal transition between homes, my impatience mounted. Even the upgrades failed to attract buyers.

When my prayers failed to yield answers, I resorted to St. Joseph for help. Our realtor had given us a small, plastic statue of St. Joseph. Superstition says that burying the statue upside down and facing the street helps to sell houses. While it sounded silly to me, impatience drove me to pluck St. Joseph out of the garage.

I remembered the cute pair of green gardening gloves I had purchased in one of my wilder moments of well intentioned gardening promises. I sighed. Everyone else finds garden so therapeutic, but not me. I donned the gloves and found the plastic statue tucked into his cardboard box.

I read the attached burial directions. They specified putting St. Joseph four inches underground. With a trowel in hand, I marched to the front yard to pick the perfect spot. I kneeled and began digging. The cold, damp soil penetrated to my achy knees, and I grimaced at the damage to my manicure despite the gloves.

My arm tired as I dug the hole, deep enough for the statue plus the four inches of dirt. My back hurt leaning over the hole, and my knees screamed for relief. Finally reaching the required depth, I stuck the statue upside down and shoved the dirt back into place. I patted the loose soil back into place.

By the following summer when we returned to the unsold Montana house, I glared at the location where I buried St. Joseph. He had failed me. When I looked closer, I noted that the spring gardeners had tilled up the soil. No doubt they dug up St. Joseph and threw him away. Just for superstitious safety, I planted another St. Joseph.

In frustration, I continued to pelt God with my prayers. I prayed more fervently. My petitions to God shifted into bargaining. Maybe God wanted me to do something in return. In high school, I had made a deal with God that if he got me through a difficult algebra test, I would say my rosary every night for a year. Maybe he wanted me to make a big donation to the church in exchange for the sale of our house.

When I ran out of bargaining ideas, I begged God to grant me the ability to trust.

TRUSTING GOD

God just didn't seem to be listening to me. Even though I begged, my pleas seemed to dissipate into the atmosphere. God didn't seem to care about my need to sell our house.

So often, we find ourselves pleading with God for help. We pray. We bargain. We do whatever it takes to make our needs known. We wait to be rescued. But no resolution appears.

Here's the pattern we employ: We pray. We listen for the solution, but nothing happens. So we pray more. Still more silence. We wait, comforting ourselves that our patience with pay off with a divine answer. We rationalize that if God really heard our prayers and really was concerned about our well being, then surely our prayers would be answered. We rely on our heartfelt sincerity and good intentions, for God should answer those. Then, we pray harder.

My Catholic upbringing described these types of prayers as supplications. They are humble petitions to the Divine for help. They are designed to alert a higher power to a need or desire of ours in hopes that it will be granted. When answers fail to arrive, our petitioning becomes more pronounced. We plea longer and harder in hopes of having our petitions bump to the top of God's to-do list.

From our point of view, God does not appear to listen when we do not receive an immediate answer to our petitions. But God does hear every prayer and answers every prayer. Maybe not in the way we expect, but answers come.

God can give three responses to our prayers:

1) God can say, "Yes." This is the answer that we are all looking for. Our troubles are over, and the situation is resolved.

2) God can say, "Not yet." We have to remember that God does not deal with time. Time is an earthly phenomenon that we try to control, sometimes to no avail. All of our prayers will be answered sooner or later, all in good time, all in God's time.

3) God can say, "I have something better in mind." This response is the tough one, calling into action our faith, trust, and hope. God knows exactly what we need and when we need it. God knows our destiny and the lessons that we are here on earth to learn. This response invites us to look with God into the Bigger Picture, the Greatest Good.

I now know that there is a Greater Plan than mine, one that I'm not privy to understanding while here on earth. With this knowledge and trust, I need to relax. I must totally give up control. I must let go of the steering wheel, knowing that I'm in good hands with God in the driver's seat. I must let God decide when it's time for our house to sell. That way, it fits into divine plans rather than human plans.

GOD'S INVITATION: TRUST

Children delight in discovering trust. They close their eyes and fling themselves into a parent's loving arms. Trust exercises for adults mimic this by using friends rather than parents. Trust-builders close their eyes and fall backwards in faith that partners will catch them before they crash to the ground.

If we can have this trust in an earthly person, a mere mortal, how much more should we be able to trust God? An all-knowing, all-powerful, and all-loving divinity surely can claim more trust from us than we allot other humans. We need to transfer the same trust we employed as children with our parents or as adults in trust-building exercises to the Divine. God will always watch out for our best providing us with what we need and a soft landing when we seem to be falling.

Sometimes our timing and God's timing are not in sync. Unfortunately, we want something now for our plans. But God has something else in mind according to His plan of eternity. Sometimes we just have to give in, to surrender to something or someone bigger than us. This is when we need to swap our prayers of supplication to prayers of surrender.

We need to shift our type of prayer. Using the Prayer of Surrender can get us started. This Prayer of

Surrender is based on four -evers: whatever, however, whenever, and forever. These four -evers serve as a template for any prayer of surrender, no matter the cause for supplication. Throughout the day, replace pleas of supplication with these:

- **Whatever:** Lord, your wish is my command. Whatever you want me to do, I accept. I say, "Yes, Coach, put me in." Bring on the people you want me to love, the situations you want me to take on, and the lessons you want me to learn. I will emulate Jesus, by saying, "Not my will, but thine be done." Whatever!

- **However:** However you choose to solve my problems, I accept your way. I know that you have the Bigger Picture that puts what is happening to me daily in a much more comprehensive life perspective. I know it will work out for the best, the way it is meant to be. However!

- **Whenever:** Lord, whenever you choose to answer my prayers, I accept your time schedule. I know that all prayers are answered, in your own good God time, giving us what we need when we need it. I will relax knowing that you have the control of the clock. Whenever!

- **Forever:** Lord I am forever grateful for the many blessings that surround me every day. The music I hear, the water that I drink, the sunlight that fills my days, and the friends who surround me with love. I will live each minute in gratitude. Forever.

We may not understand exactly what each situation brings to us, but be assured that as God's treasured children, we will be loved and cared for. Practice surrendering to His will with the 4-evers.

PRAYER

Dear Lord, I know I am loved and cared for by an all-knowing Creator, giving me exactly what I need for my journey in perfect timing.

6

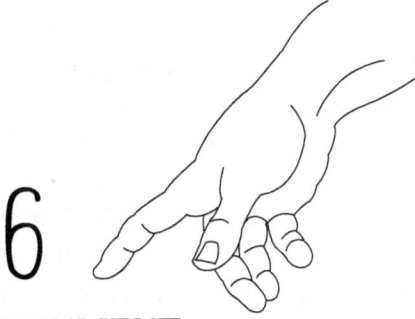

GAINING DISCERNMENT

Discernment is also one of the last things we learn, when we feel our paths diverge and we must separate from our mentors in order to stay true to ourselves.
—Anne Hill, The Baby and the Bathwater

Joe and I stripped down in the TSA checkpoint in the Phoenix airport. Whipping off belts, shoes, and jewelry, we stood in line for the scanner. Dressed in my plain black slacks and simple shirt, devoid of any adornment whatsoever, I bounded through the metal detector. As usual, I smugly waited for Joe. With two artificial knees, he had to go through the mandatory pat down.

Because Joe and I are such soul mates with no one to interject alternative behaviors into our scheme, we always arrive at the airports early. We often arrive so early that two flights depart from our gate before ours even arrives. We both agree that we would rather wait than be rushed and worried. To pass the time, we eat. Settling into a comfy booth we ordered breakfast getting out the iPads to pass the hours until departure. We camped out ordering more coffee to justify our extended table stay. We even ordered a third round.

By the time we board the plane and the flight attendants served up drinks, I had to beeline for the bathroom at the rear of the plane to pay for my sin of drinking too much coffee. I was not the only one with the same bladder condition. The five-person line extended back into the aisle, where I struck up a conversation with a couple sitting there. Chit-chatting about the weather and our destinations, I passed the time waiting in line until a jolt tossed me off balance. But my hands on the seat tops kept me from falling.

In less than a minute, the captain's voice shot across the intercom: "Please return to your seats. We are hitting some turbulence." The fasten seat belt sign beeped on. I pursed my lips in consternation. With all the coffee that morning, I needed to use the restroom now. I wasn't sure I could wait.

Despite my physical need, I did as I was told. I marched back to my seat and clipped into my seatbelt. While squirming around in my seat, safely belted in, I turned around with a longing glance toward the restroom. Much to my dismay, I saw the other four people still standing in line. They either didn't hear the captain's voice of authority or didn't care to obey. I flounced around in my seat, disgusted with my guilt sponge obedience. My automatic compulsion to obey authoritative commands kept me squirming in my seat instead of rejoining the line.

Joe looked at me. I shook my head and rolled my eyes, muttering, "I'm such a guilt sponge."

GAINING DISCERNMENT

Guilt sponges soak up the wishes of the others and try to please authority. As a good girl, raised in a strict

Catholic environment, I learned to make decisions based on guilt and fear. The convent reinforced this guilt sponge behavior by demanding unquestioning obedience. It is so automatic with me that decades later, I still behave the same way rather than thinking for myself.

Some of those people in the airplane bathroom line who turned a deaf ear to our pilot may have been raised with the same discipline of heeding obedience to organized religions. But they apparently moved beyond the compulsion to obey without question. During my spiritual journey, I have discovered that many fellow spiritual sojourners were right along beside me searching for spirituality minus the guilt and unquestioning obedience.

The Pew Research Center has documented a growing movement that expresses dissent with organized religion. Their most recent survey on religion in America tallied up more people checking the term "none" from the list of religions. Failing to find the appropriate religious pigeonhole to check–Catholic, Protestant, Islam–responders go for "none of the above."

The survey also showed that many of the none-of-the-above checkers still felt they were spiritual. This group has been referred to as the Spiritual But Not Religious (SBNRs). SBNRs do not hold one specific spiritual theology. Looking outside one traditional religion, they ascribe to all religions containing some wisdom, but no one religion containing all wisdom. For my guilt sponge soaked life, this point of view provided fresh waves of insight and relief.

Various authors have cited that SBNRs tally up to around 30 million people. Numbers have doubled in the past decade.

One of my blog readers wrote to me about this very subject, passing on what she had heard on the radio. People come to church to find God, but they only find religion. Sometimes people get so caught up in the trappings of religion they get lost in the checklist of what is expected of them. Religion focuses on performing rites, rituals, and saying prayers, novenas, and confession. It leaves the more personal relationship with Spirit as secondary. Religious practices designed to bring us closer to God may even get in the way of connecting with the Spirit.

Sometimes all the rules are at odds with our evolving belief systems. Practices that once served a meaningful purpose lose their importance in meeting our needs today. Religion may be one stepping-stone, but we must not trip up on the stones making one religion the only path. SBNRs are taking responsibility, making spiritual decisions that resonate with them, not waiting for directions from the pulpit.

My journey has gone from Catholic nun to spiritual none. I have woven my beliefs with those that I grew up with. While I still find myself automatically obeying authority, I give myself permission to shed the guilt sponge thinking in favor of a healthier approach.

GOD'S INVITATION: DISCERNMENT

To avoid being a guilt sponge requires discernment. Discernment is the ability to judge with insight. It gives us a wise perception of a situation. Using discernment, we tap in to deeper soul knowledge.

In religious circles, discernment is the method of learning about God's desire for us. Tapping into the inner core with discernment can direct us to vocations–to serve God as a priest, nun, single life, married life, or some other realm.

An old soul is a person who has an uncanny sense of knowing the truth and the ability to get the heart of a problem. Old souls do not get caught up in the derailing details, but seem to sense between the lines. They understand experiences and can project outcomes. This ability to discern is a useful tool especially with nonstop information pulling us all ways politically, religiously, and personally.

Discernment is a prerequisite for wisdom. Discernment sorts truth.

So how can we gain discernment?

Discernment can be a gift. But we can practice tactics to build discernment. We can increase the ability to get to the heart of the matter. We can develop the skill to look beyond stumbling blocks to see the bigger true picture.

We come into this world with an inner counselor or guidance system. This inner GPS can be God's Pulley System. It can tug us in a certain direction. Emotions and feelings provide us with unbiased, untainted, and untouched evidence. Practice listening to gut feelings for first hand information that you will need along your way. These gut instincts have directional pull.

We can take a lesson from the child's game of Marco Polo. Usually played in a swimming pool, one person calls out, "Marco," while the other swimmers respond with "Polo" with eyes supposedly shut. As the call and response continues, the Polo swimmers splash toward the voice to tag or catch Marco.

The same concept applies to us, listening and picking up on God's vibrations leading us to our true calling. Feeling blinded ourselves, we seek vibrations or light along our way. In a way, God calls out "Marco," and we respond with "Polo," honing in on what God wants us to do.

In order to develop discernment to detect the voice of God, we can employ several tactics daily. These are small skill-builders that may lead us eventually to bigger a-ha Moments.

- Develop the habit of checking in with yourself. In the midst of any activity during the day, stop and see how you are feeling, or what pull you are experiencing. Maybe you are being pulled to an afternoon nap, or perhaps you need a walk outside in fresh air. Discernment is built around your inner connection.

- Pray to ask God for enlightenment. Often times being quiet, reflecting and praying about a circumstance brings clarity itself.

- Try to see situations or beliefs from more than one side. Know that there is more than one right answer. Stay non-judgmental in sizing up a situation, person, or circumstance.

- Seek out trusted friends or experts in the field for wise counsel. With an outside perspective, true confidants can widen the scope of our vision.

- Get used to swimming upstream, stepping away

from the accepted norm. You might be the only one with this view. You may not fit in with your peers or the popular vote. You might go against authority to follow your own conscience rather than someone else's directives. Be open to being led to see the authentic or the obscure that others may miss. Be strong enough to sustain those views.

Getting in touch with your wise inner counselor will develop a confidence and source for your discernment, leading you on your intended path.

PRAYER

Dear Lord, please help me to discern what comes my way. Let me see your truth in situations and lead me to see the Bigger Picture.

Guarding Your Self-Love

7
EMBRACING FAILURES

It is impossible to live without failing at something, unless you live so cautiously that you might as well not have lived at all, in which case you have failed by default.
—J. K. Rowling

I sunk into the lawn chair in my parent's back yard, a complete failure. As the oldest of five children, I was supposed to be a good behavior model for my younger siblings. Instead, at 38 years old, a cloud of depression swamped me when I returned to live with my parents.

My younger sisters followed the normal path of college, marriage, and child rearing, fitting right into expected societal behavior. I followed a different path.

Heeding a special calling, I chose a vocation to serve God as a nun. My dad had urged me to go to college first, and then if I still wanted to become a nun, I could. Thinking that I knew better, I argued for the convent first. But after seven years of service, I returned home to California having failed at finding the happiness I sought.

After leaving the security of the cloistered walls, the outside life seemed forbidding. I was used to living in a tight-knit community. Instead of the vows of poverty, chastity, and obedience being the preferred codes of behavior, this new outside world appeared lavish, plastic, and competitive.

Eager to fit in to cultural norms, I married within 14 months of departing the convent. From all outside appearances, I looked normal with the perfect husband, perfect house, and perfect vacations. I partied with my husband's friends as my own, seeming to be the co-ed that I wasn't. When happiness eluded me once again, I sought a divorce.

Nineteen years after entering the convent, two failed marriages–one to God and one to Mark–hung on me like large Fs on report cards. Only instead of failing school classes, I'd failed at life. I slunk back home again to hide my shame.

In the back yard, clothed in my failures, I collapsed into the lawn chair to talk with my dad. He quizzed me about my choices for entering the convent and staying in a doomed marriage.

"Why did you stay so long in both situations that weren't working for you?" he asked.

I looked down at my feet. "All I tried to do my whole life is to please you and make you proud of me, and all I did was to let you down," I choked out the words. Pent up tears unleashed the admission that had burdened me for years. But I hadn't pleased anyone. Not even myself.

Instead, I had assumed a heavy burden of responsibility and striving to be perfect to please both my earthly father and heavenly father. Failing them, I felt like a broken china doll with shards of my life shattered on the floor.

My failure at life led to self-loathing. Self-hatred brought me face-to-face with the all-important question: How could God love me when I didn't even love myself?

EMBRACING FAILURES

Success, not failure, was our mantra growing up. We strove to be perfect. We aimed to be the perfect family with the perfectly behaved children. If we did happen to fail, we went to confession to wash away our sins. Our education, upbringing, and vision geared us for the fast track to success rather than failure.

Take a look at the contrast with Sara Blakely, the spunky young entrepreneur who started the acclaimed worldwide company of Spanx that designs shape wear for women and men. In an Australian interview, Sara shared one very important factor contributing to her rise in the business world. Once a week her father would quiz her brother and her around the dinner table. Her father would ask them each how they had failed during that week and what they had learned.

Sara grew up with the habit of failure. She gained a powerful tool in learning to take missteps and turn them into stepping-stones for success. Contrary to Sara, I avoided the habit of embracing failure. In fact, I never learned how to use failure for my gain.

We need to shift the paradigm of failure. We need to incorporate this incremental step of failure, embracing it as part of the normal path to a goal. Putting judgment aside, we need to see how everything works together for the best.

In the 1970s, I read an article in *Cosmopolitan* magazine entitled "What's Right with Mr. Wrong." In it, a 40-year-old woman shared her dating story. She addressed an audience that believed that something was wrong with women who at 30 years old were not married with two children, a perfect husband, and beautiful home with a white picket fence.

But this woman shifted the failure paradigm. Rather than viewing her life as lacking, she treasured what each of her failed relationships had gifted her. Each man in some way had enriched her life. If it hadn't been for Paul, she would never had been exposed to opera. If it hadn't been for Bill, she would have missed out on how to ride a motorcycle. Each of her failed relationships contributed to the mosaic of the person that she now was. Each man had a positive influence leading to her wholeness.

Today, we can hardly get away from being judged against successes. Magazine stories laud the best: Top 10 Doctors, the Man of Your Dreams, Five-Star Restaurants, and Woman of the Year. We match ourselves up against these winners.

With this competitive element, there is no room for the failure-learning-retry scenario. We need to put judgment on the back shelf and appreciate just who we are, where we are, and what we are. We need to ditch the words "should," "must," and "ought." We need to throw out the guilt when we do not follow the prescribed norm. We may all be on the same journey but not necessarily on the same road. We need to honor our own path of learning life's lesson.

GOD'S INVITATION: HONOR THYSELF

Honor thy father and thy mother, the commandment reads. I applied the concept of honor always outside myself: respecting my parents and elders, paying regards to hosts, avoiding selfishness, and considering others before myself. But honor was measured by somebody else's standard of behavior rather than my own.

God extends an invitation, a G-vite, for us to honor ourselves. It means that we are to acknowledge and love the unique person that we are called to be, respecting our own personal journey. We even need to respect the bumps in the road.

To honor thyself means to believe in yourself, your beauty, your potential, your uniqueness, and your path. You have your own standards and your own boundaries, taking full responsibility for your integrity and values. You are led by your strength and operate from the good within. You are the only person with your gifts, talents, and characteristics. You are the only person who can fulfill your mission. You are the one and only who can sing your song.

Sammy Davis, Jr. gained fame for his theme song, "I've Got to Be Me." While the words can fuel a big ego, they can also grant permission to listen to your gut and follow it. It gives you permission to swim upstream or to dance to a different drummer.

In understanding your destiny and sense of purpose, don't be tempted to fall into working solely to please others and meet their expectations. Cultural norms, social responsibilities, and religious rules can throw guilt on us for not doing it their way, making us feel like we have failed in some way. In addition to outside influences, we have our own inner code to adhere to and when we don't measure up, we deem ourselves failures for not meeting the success standards that we have set for ourselves. Because this burden of responsibility weighs so heavily upon us, we need to be gentle with our self-judgment.

To assist in honoring thyself, I suggest a simple old school procedure–the permission slip. When your stomach shoots out darts of failure, get out a special notebook, maybe like a doctor's prescription pad. With pen in hand, give yourself a formal break, permission to screw up. Use these words for starters:

This slip gives Patty official permission to fail at _____.

She has learned _____.

She knows that this misstep is a stepping-stone to success.

Writing it down can bring more awareness to the important part that failure plays in our growth. Babies don't walk on their first attempt. Toddlers don't speak in complete sentences immediately. Why should learning our life lessons be any different than trying to master riding a wave on a surfboard for the first time or scoring an ace serve on the first tennis set?

Give yourself permission to follow your heart, putting

judgment aside. Honor your own instincts in a loving response to God's G-vite.

PRAYER

Dear Lord, help me honor the wonderful person that you made in me, with all my wonderful talents. May I always use my missteps as stepping-stones to love myself as much as you do.

8
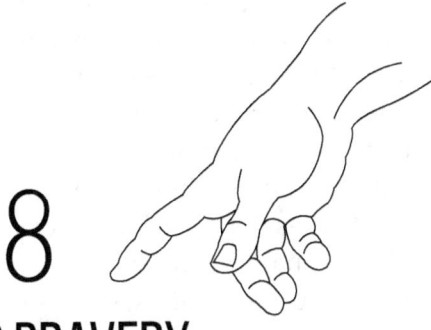

SUMMONING BRAVERY

Life shrinks or expands in proportion to one's courage.
—Anaïs Nin

"Sure, that would be great. Joe and I are really looking forward to seeing you." Hanging up the phone, I ended the familiar booking conversation for summer visitors at our Montana home. I penned the dates on my calendar.

July looked full. Grabbing my pink highlighter, I began marking off the number of overnight visitors we expected during the 31 days in that month. Bright pink highlights filled the month. I counted up 27 days with overnight houseguests. The four remaining free days in July were not even consecutive.

My stomach flip-flopped. During the previous summer, we were deluged with visitors. I swore to limit the number of visitors this summer, but without success. Montanans claimed two seasons: winter and guests. My calendar attested to that theory. Our housekeeper, acting as guest bedroom manager, even joked about our home being the Kogi B&B. "We might need a small business license!" she lobbed.

I mentally checked off my responsibilities: event orchestration, scheduling excursions into Glacier Park, meal planning, grocery shopping, restaurant reservations, river rafting arrangements, securing golf tee times, preparing the guest beds, and baking breakfast casseroles. Shouldering the burden of ensuring that each of our friends would experience the best of Montana, I strove to look nonchalant about the impending crush of visitors.

One of our Montana friends who had been through this summer onslaught too many times before resorted to guarding her precious summer months by including a short list enclosed in her Christmas cards. In addition to holiday wishes, she enclosed a card enumerating of all the hotels, motels, inns, and B&Bs in the area with their addresses and phone numbers. Her note read, "Whitefish is a lovely place to visit, with activities for both summer and winter. We would love to see you any season. Give us a call, and we'd love to meet you for dinner!"

My friend took control of her own happiness. Her tactic worked. She still saw visitors, but without the stress of being their concierge, guide, cook, and housekeeper.

Glancing at the 95 percent of my days in July that were booked with guests, I groaned. But rather than suffer the guilt of disappointing even one guest by cancelling our availability, I chose to accept all guests. I took a deep breath to face the summer.

SUMMONING BRAVERY

Afraid to suffer the pangs of guilt at disappointing others, I placated the needs of others rather than my own. My avoidance of disappointing others kept me from stepping on toes, but at the expense of myself. I so often feel like I need to say "No," but instead spew out the words "I'll be glad to."

My predicament demonstrates the need for bravery. I needed to be my own hero, ready to disappoint people and being okay with shouldering that feeling of letting others down. My lack of bravery built my own personal prison, confining my own wants, needs, and desires to accommodate others wishes.

I'm born to please. Those like me who are firmly grounded on the foundation of pleasing construct their personal prisons. We want others to like us, regard us as team players, and rest assured they can always count on us, no matter what the situation.

All of our decision-making skills revolve around these crippling internal motivations. With people pleasing as the foundation, we construct four prison walls with debilitating behaviors. In order to please others, we strive to be perfect and to perform as expected. These are two of the walls. Here's the logic we use:

- **Striving to be perfect:** If I'm the perfect little girl, then no one will criticize me. Everyone will like me. I will make everyone happy, and things will run smoothly.

- **Striving to perform as expected:** Even though I don't enjoy water skiing, my husband does, so I'll go along to ski anyway. I hate that particular Thanksgiving dressing, but my mother-in-law is counting on it, so I'll make it.

Then, here's where things get silly. In order to shore up our perfection and performance, we add two more walls to the prison. We rationalize to survive. We pretend and procrastinate to avoid facing reality and how unhappy pleasing others makes us. Take a look at these examples of how we rationalize through adopting what isn't real:

- **Adopting pretend views:** My family situation is perfect. My husband is successful, and all my children are gifted, honor-roll material. I ignore what isn't successful.

- **Adopting procrastination:** If I told my husband how I really felt, it would ruin our anniversary celebration, so I'll tell him at a better time. I'll lose those five pounds after my birthday.

With the focus on pleasing others, we build prison walls around ourselves. The walls limit our gain of personal freedom and happiness. If we don't take control of our own happiness, someone else will take control for us.

We need to summon our own bravery. We must seek the courage to disappoint others. What others think of us is none of our business.

GOD'S INVITATION: BRAVERY

We don't meet God when things are easy. Hardship is the portal to divine connection and personal growth. That is especially true when God invites us to acquire bravery.

The G-vite of bravery calls to our deepest nerve. It summons us to believe in ourselves along our personal journey. We must dig deep down to live fearlessly in order to disappoint others when we must. It takes a lot of courage to say, "No."

Bravery is not acting with a lack of fear, but a faith-filled determination to proceed in spite of internal rumblings and doubt. We were taught it was selfish not to think of others first. We were considered self-absorbed when watching out for number one. No one ever taught us how to take care of ourselves. We were put on this earth to serve others, but in order to care our best for others, we must take care of ourselves. It's natural to find that caring for ourselves and seeking our own wants comes with difficulty.

Cultivating this bravery, and being willing to disappoint others takes practice. Start practicing with smaller ways to say "No" and build up to bigger ways. Use the following three steps as a menu for building from shorter to longer and terser to more friendly declines.

- **First:** Start with just saying "No." By itself, the word "No" forms a complete sentence. This small two-letter word is very powerful, but sometimes very difficult to choke out.

- **Second:** Build to adding a few more words. More words create a little softer landing. Expand the decline with something like "No thanks, I'll have to pass," or "That won't work for me right now." Stop with those brief statements. No need to add any thing more to appear more plausible or more convincing. Avoid rattling on with excuses or explanations of why it won't work. Additional explanations weaken our resolve and begin to appear as excuses.

- **Third:** At a book signing for my first book *A Change of Habit* at an "I Can Do It!" conference, Hay House presenter Cheryl Richardson suggested a comfortable, easy format for saying no. Offer a polite thank you comment, say "No," and then close with an upbeat positive message.

Using Cheryl's three-step pattern, we can elaborate with the No Sandwich visual. Think of the meat in the sandwich as the word "No" slid in between two slices of complimentary bread.

The conversation would go something like this:

"Patty, would you like to take on the role of the presidency next year for the school's PTA?" says Virginia.

"Oh, Virginia, I'm so honored that you would consider me for that leadership position. I think I'll have to pass. Thanks for thinking of me, but I know you will find someone with great leadership skills that I will be glad to support in any way that I can."

Let's dissect the three parts of the answer.

The first sentence is one slice of complimentary bread. "I'm so honored that you would consider me for that leadership position."

The second sentence is the slice of meat. "I think I'll have to pass." It conveys the word "No," the hearty meat of the message.

The third sentence is the other slice of complimentary bread. "Thanks for thinking of me, but I know you will find someone with great leadership skills that I will be glad to support in any way that I can." This adds on a positive ending.

With the No Sandwich firmly in place as part of our repertoires, we won't be caught off guard stammering when approached with a less than favorable request. Using the No Sandwich will buy us some valuable think time.

PRAYER

Dear Lord, help me to love myself as much as you love me. Thank you for the guidance and support when I need to be brave to say "No" to protect my own happiness. I know that I'm divinely guided.

9

BUILDING COMPASSION

Love and compassion are necessities, not luxuries. Without them, humanity cannot survive.
—Dalai Lama XIV, *The Art of Happiness*

"Good job!" the computer voice heralded my play. The slot machine game on my iPad entertained me while I waited in the restaurant for Joe to show up. With each bet, the slot reels twirled until they landed.

I felt like a slot slut hooked on my game. The clinking of the change, the whirring clicks of the spinning reels, and the sirens of being a winner whined loud enough for others to hear. Placing my bet, I crossed my fingers and eyed each reel as it dramatically came to a landing. Three matching bonus boxes or scatter icons indicated that I won. Three matching bonus boxes entitled me to five spins or the opportunity to try my luck in the bonus game, where I could demonstrate skill in avoiding vampires and navigating mazes to find buried treasure for extra points.

I bet 50 coins. The spin won me 20 coins. My shoulders dropped in disappointment. "Great spin," the game barked like a carnival hawker. Without hesitation, the game reinforced my bet. The fact that I'd just lost 30 coins didn't matter.

I wagered 100 coins. When the reels settled, I won 40 coins on the spin. "Good job!" the game encouraged me onward regardless of the amount of coins I had just lost. Addicted to the game, I kept betting and losing. But with each loss, recorded comments spit out, "This is craaa-ZEE. You are incredible. You are awesome!" As the game proceeded, I saw myself as a loser because I wagered more coins than I won back. But the game encouraged me to keep playing with uplifting responses to my losses. No matter what I did, or what stupid play failed, the game did not reprimand me. It did not blame; it did not throw any guilt my way. No matter what happened, it praised me.

The game knew I was really a winner, despite the coin count. It had faith in my abilities, and I felt its support. Even though my total coin count diminished, the positive response from the game made me feel better about losing, thus compelling me to spin the reels once more.

BUILDING COMPASSION

If we could have the game voice laud us through our difficulties, we would feel so much better. Instead, we beat ourselves up. We chastise ourselves for not meeting expectations. We deem that we should have been smarter, faster, or should have known better. Failing to meet self-expectations or expectations from others gives us fodder to reprimand ourselves. We then feel guilt because we feel we deserved the reprimands.

We replay a negative tape in our minds: We are not enough. We are not thin enough, kind enough, industrious enough, or disciplined enough. This self-talk builds up guilty feelings for being such a failure.

I often find my self-talk bordering on abusive. While I would choose to avoid a person who said these things to me, I submit willingly to listen to myself spew negativity:

- I should have kept my mouth shut.
- I knew that she would react this way, and I still went ahead.
- How stupid of me.
- I could kick myself for doing that.
- How dumb!
- I shouldn't have done that.
- That was so stupid.
- I am an idiot!

The endless rerun of these negative tapes erodes our self-confidence. As our self-confidence washes away, so does our happiness.

Instead of bashing ourselves with negative self-talk, we need to heed the lesson from the slot machine game. We need to turn our negative self-talk into words that boost self-confidence and compassion. We can take the same words from the slot machine game to show us how to develop positive reinforcement.

Instead of self-talk based in loathing our own behavior, we need to make our own tape recording of positive reinforcing messages. The Spirit universally grants us love and total acceptance. So it follows that our self-talk tapes need to play messages of love and acceptance from God:

- You are so wonderful!
- I am with you wherever you go, whatever you do.
- I will never let you down.
- You are an amazing reflection of the Divine.
- You are a perfect creation.

Especially during stressful times, when we fall short of expectations, we need to hit the off button for negativity. Instead, we need to hit the positive play key. We can even cast positive reinforcement in other terms:

- I gave it a shot; next time I will succeed.
- This is only a misstep and a stepping-stone on the road to success.
- This is not a failure because I learned something.
- I am all that I am supposed to be right now.

Positive reinforcement of total love and acceptance can promote a healthy spiritual life. It can build self-confidence and happiness even during trying times. We can be winners in spite of what is happening around us.

Next time I play the slots, I know that I'm merely getting new material for my affirmations! I will copy the game voice for positive self-talk. We can all play our own winning tapes and know we can't lose in this lifetime.

GOD'S INVITATION: COMPASSION

God invites us to engage in sympathy for ourselves, as well as others. Physical, emotional, or spiritual needs can ignite compassion. They are a call to action, inciting us to reach out to ourselves or others with support.

Building compassion for others begins with self-love. Knowing how to nurture ourselves in times of need enables us to approach others in awareness and knowledge.

We all grew up with the spiritual lesson of compassion. We were taught, "Love your neighbor as yourself." But most of us never stop to define how to love ourselves nor consider the relationship between loving ourselves and loving others.

Consider how negative self-talk works. I beat myself up with negative self-talk, but I would never speak those harsh words to my neighbor. If I wouldn't speak to my neighbor in those negative words, why am I so willing to use words of condemnation on myself? Hopefully, my treatment of my fellow humans is not the same as how I treat myself. Perhaps we should twist the old commandment around to make the point clearer: I should love myself as well as I love my neighbor!

As I learn social media under my coaching mentors, I experience cycles of ups and downs in the learning curve. I fumble for forgotten passwords and lost user names. I wander around aimlessly on the web in search of answers. I feel like a complete failure. I want to berate myself, "How could I be so slow? Others pick these things up so fast."

But my coaches take a more positive approach. They encourage me onward, "Sweetie, don't worry; we'll find that password. You'll get this." With these comforting terms, my shoulders drop, the knot in my stomach unwinds, and my headache subsides. What do I hear? I do not hear any judgment. Only encouragement, acceptance, and motivation come through loud and clear. My coaches deliver compassion in positive words.

So how do we learn compassion? In order to engage in the response of compassion for ourselves and others, we must drop one component—criticism. Many of us were raised to judge. We learned criticism as an element of evaluation. We learned to deem things, people, or actions as good or bad. While black-and-white thinking has its place in intellectual development, constant evaluation of ourselves can build unhappiness, negativity, and shallow thinking. Nonstop judging ourselves and others takes us down a negative road.

To build the G-vite of compassion, we must choose the positive road instead. We must step out of our judgmental selves. One method to build compassion for ourselves is to remove the judgment and emotions from how we see our own actions. To do so, we can recast the predicament as a newspaper article. Here's how to do it:

- Pretend you are writing about your actions in your local newspaper.
- Write a short newspaper article about what happened using third person instead of first person ("The woman" instead of "I.")
- Report just the facts: who was present, where it took place, when the incident occurred, and what exactly transpired.
- Use unbiased words with no words of condemnation or judgment.

- Be objective; remove all emotion from your writing.

Once you have written the piece, let it sit for an hour while you do something else. Then, go back to read your article. Read it while conjuring compassion for the woman in the story. Most of us find that we are reading about commonalities between all people.

To respond to the invitation of compassion, let's work to remove critical judgment from our daily lives. Get used to seeing your life as an observer and not the judge. Rather than replaying emotions that stem from harsh judgment of ourselves, we need to recast our mistakes with detachment to eliminate the emotional drain.

Remember: You are a winner. By creating compassion for ourselves, we can develop compassion for others. Through that compassion, we can fulfill our destinies.

PRAYER

Dear Lord, I know your love for me is not dependent on what I do or don't do. Help me to love myself as you do with compassion and understanding.

PART II

TRUSTING G-VITES TO SURVIVE ADVERSITY

Moving On Through Hardships

10
DEVELOPING HONESTY

Honesty is the first chapter in the book of wisdom.
—Thomas Jefferson

As the elevator door opened on the 11th floor, my knees weakened, my breath quickened, and the all too familiar stomach spasms started again. "What in the hell was I doing here?" I berated myself as I made my way down the hall to Dr. Chapin's office.

After my divorce from a 12-year failed marriage, happiness still eluded me. I sought professional help with a psychiatrist. As a guilt sponge, my entire life drew my attention outward, gaining my approval from others. Perceiving the wants and needs of others became my specialty. I practiced being perfect, following the rules at home and complying with the commandments of the church. But my choices and behaviors failed to lead to happiness.

Mustering my courage, I walked into the waiting room filled with outdated magazines and two other patients. I wondered what their problems were. In the convent we were accustomed to a practice called Custody of the Eyes. This exercise instructed nuns to keep their eyes focused downward rather than making eye contact as an outward sign of humility. At last, some of my convent training paid off keeping me in my own little world of private thoughts while biding my waiting time.

After entering Dr. Chapin's office, I squirmed in my seat as she sat in silence behind her desk reviewing my paperwork. Removing her cheater reading glasses, she began, "I see here that you recently went through a divorce."

"Yes, I did," I admitted, folding my hands to hide the shaking.

"Well, tell me how you feel about this whole divorce?"

"I'm fine."

"That's good, but what exactly do you feel?"

Geez, no one had ever asked that of me. "I'm not sure what I feel," I squirmed again.

"Are you sad?"

"I might be."

"Are you angry?"

"Maybe."

"Are you mad?"

"I just don't know." I choked back tears. I had no idea of how I felt. After all those years of suppressing my own feelings, only caring about what others were thinking of me, numbness shrouded my own emotions. I had lost touch with myself. Success at accommodating the wishes of others came at the expense of myself.

DEVELOPING HONESTY

Thomas Jefferson had it right. Honesty is the first chapter in the Book of Wisdom. Here I sat in the shrink's office baffled at the first chapter of my own life. I could not answer Dr. Chapin's questions because I could not be honest with myself. To survive despondency after my divorce, I needed to start being honest with myself.

Often, we behave like the myth of the ostrich. Tiny ostrich heads look like they are buried in sand when they peck around for food or turn eggs in a hole, which gave rise to the myth that ostriches bury their heads when scared. They really don't bury their heads in sand, but the myth persists because we do behave like the ostrich myth. When faced with adversity, we jam our heads down into the sand instead of facing the truth with honesty. We bury our heads to avoid facing reality. In my case, I buried my own emotions in the sand in order to meet the demands of others.

We also avoid honesty in the face of adversity by creating make-believe worlds. We kid ourselves with denial. We blame others. We play if-only games. In fact, we are experts at avoiding honesty. Guilt, fear, or our need for security makes us create our own illusions. We pretend our lives are okay when they are not. We claim things are fine when they are not. We go to great lengths to deny that we feel sad, angry, or mad because these are scary emotions that can whirl out of control. Since I bought into behaving like the perfect daughter, perfect nun, and perfect wife, that illusion of perfection demanded that I avoid personal emotions that could explode my world with human faults. I excelled at denial.

We've all heard the phrase "brutally honest." That's precisely how honesty can strike us. It is brutal. Looking squarely at a situation with honesty can push us out of our comfort zone. We may have to admit to owning scary emotions and then deal with them. Yikes! But in order to face the adversities in front of us, we must be brutally honest to see where we really sit. We cannot move forward to alleviate sadness until we admit to the melancholy. We cannot dispel anger until we recognize the depth of its corrosion on us. Facing those emotions takes brutal honesty.

To face one's own feelings starts with taking time to breathe. Breathing allows a pause to summon courage. Then, we can open ourselves to face the truth of the situation. It requires vulnerability. But we are divinely guided through this adversity. When the tough work of brutal honesty is done in facing the adversity, we can then grow through the adversity.

Naming our emotions is key. It sounds so simple, but naming our emotions gives recognition to their existence. Naming them also demands brutal honesty with ourselves. In turn, naming emotions begins to diminish their power. Naming them lessens their weight on us. Psychologist Dan Siegel uses this tactic for children having meltdowns. He refers to the process as "name it to tame it." But the process works for adults, too. We can name our emotions to begin to tame them. When we honestly face what we are really feeling, then we can take on the adversity in front of us.

Growth occurs at the bitter edge. It occurs when we are pushed out of our comfort zone. We need to inch up to honesty, no matter how difficult it may be. The rewards will be surprising.

GOD'S INVITATION: HONESTY

Honesty begins within. Being honest with ourselves is paramount to building true happiness. With that honesty comes a freedom from deceit that leads to candor, genuineness, and integrity that spill out into our relationships with others.

How can we become honest with ourselves? Start listening inside. Don't listen to the mind chattering away with messages of what you should do or what you ought to have done. Instead, take some quiet time and just BE. Feel what your body is trying to tell you. Let emotions surface.

The process requires quiet and inward focus, a skill we must learn. This means starting with only a few minutes of just being. The Five Times a Day Challenge can help. To be successful with the challenge, designate those five times in the morning, setting computer alarms if necessary as reminders of the task.

At the appointed time, pause whatever you are doing. Sit down. Breathe slowly and deeply. Clear your mind, and check in with yourself. See if you can get in touch with what you feel. Try to name the emotion.

After five minutes, quit. Go back to what you were doing. As you continue to take the Five Times a Day

Challenge, you can extend the time allotted to check in with yourself.

If stymied, try turning attention to bodily hints: headaches, nervous twitches, stomach pains, tense muscles. Focus on breathing through those. Ask those physical symptoms what they are trying to tell you about what is really happening inside. These can be clues to emotions, for often our emotions manifest in physical symptoms. Tense muscles can be signs of pent up anger. Headaches can speak to stress. Stomach aches can point to swallowing emotions.

Let your own Inner Counselor work as your guiding light. Your emotions act as the window to your soul. These feelings speak to your truest desires. The knot in your stomach, the hesitation in your smile, and the resistance to say yes once again are all prods moving you in the direction of truth and personal growth. God wants us to feel our way along our journey in this school called Life.

As you name your emotions and what you are feeling, that emotion can begin to lose power. It's like a balloon that suddenly has the air let out. It grows smaller. Once named, the weight of the emotion also becomes lighter. It is defined. It is no longer a huge, amorphous unknown monster. Because it is defined, it is easier to face. Once your Five Times a Day Challenge lets you tap into your emotions and you name them, then you have acquired the G-vite of honesty. Use that honesty to face the adversity before you.

By listening to your emotions, the inner voice, and the quiet tugging of your heartstrings, the Spirit will lead you. Quiet your mind, listen to your gut, breathe, feel your innards, and those vibes will lead your heart to guilt-free happiness. Don't miss out on your own life.

PRAYER

Dear Lord, as I start being honest with myself, I know that I have your support. Help me to face myself, know myself, and love myself as you do.

11
INCREASING PERSEVERANCE

If you are going through hell, keep going.
—Winston Churchill

On Friday afternoon, the whine of the school buses pulling out of the elementary school parking lot played as music to my ears. As the principal of the school, I whirled in perpetual motion through each week with little time to catch my breath. I yearned for the weekend to relax.

The stack of mail on my desk served as an invitation finally to collapse in my chair. As I shuffled through the pre-opened envelopes, I caught sight of an unusual sealed envelope. After my secretary sorted the mail, she usually opened all the envelopes for me with her eyes first on matters to be considered.

This strange piece of mail bore a stamp marked private. I scanned the return address for any clues to its contents. "Attorneys at Law," it said. My stomach tightened. After digging in my desk for a letter opener, I sliced open the package, pulled out a sheaf of papers, and scanned the cover letter. My breathing ceased. My heart thumped.

The letter notified me that a lawsuit was personally naming me at fault in an action for one million dollars! "This must be a mistake," I thought. "I didn't do anything wrong. I work hard to follow the rules." My world collapsed while I tried to put all the pieces of the lawsuit together.

My school secretary had initiated the lawsuit, naming the school district, the superintendent, and me at fault. Each party was liable for a million dollars.

"What?!" I reread the words to correct my misunderstanding. But there they were in black and white. My secretary initiated this litigation. She was the woman that I went to bat for with the school leadership team during the interviewing process. We worked side by side in the administrative office, rushing to meet deadlines, accommodating irate parents, and nursing sick children for four years. I thought of the two of us as comrades in the trenches together. We exchanged gifts on Christmas and birthdays. I honored her on Secretary's Day. We labored together, lunched together, and laughed together.

I thought I knew her. I liked her. I thought she liked me. But her lawsuit yanked me off balance. Sucker-punched in one swoop, all of my faith in my personal and professional abilities tumbled into an abyss. My hands trembled. Fear flooded over me, sorrow wrapped my heart, and bile filled my stomach. My whole body shook.

BUILDING PERSEVERANCE

That Friday at school, I felt like life was punched right out of me. No matter how supporting people tried to be, their words provided no respite. The district attorneys reassured me that it was a frivolous lawsuit. I lived on emotional eggshells for years with tears poised to flood at the inopportune times.

My administrative courses attempted to prepare us for the pressures of the job. But this was far beyond our scope of study. With my self-confidence on the brink of collapse, I began to rethink my career in administration. After all, if I couldn't stand the excessive heat, I should exit the kitchen.

The lawsuit dragged on for seven years, including a three-year appeal. Every time I received a copy of communication in the case from that same address, it came with a punch in the gut. By the end of the lawsuit, I had given up my career. The lawsuit was eventually thrown out, as our lawyers had asserted it would be.

We all face adversity, whether it be physical, mental, or emotional. The loss of a child, incurable illness, a miscarriage of injustice, the death of a loved one, or financial ruin can take a toll on us. No matter the cause of suffering, they all have similar components that test our endurance.

1. **We feel out of control.** Things are out of our hands. There is absolutely nothing that we can do to mitigate what is happening. We feel bound up in a straight jacket with no way out.

2. **We feel we don't deserve the suffering.** We see it as unfair. We question, "Why me?"

3. **We endure long suffering.** Sometimes, these tests spread out over years. The pain never seems to

go away. Time does not seem to heal all wounds.

4. **We wallow in hopelessness.** We hear no answers. No one can help us. A feeling of isolation or despair rocks our emotional wellbeing.

"That which doesn't kill us, makes us stronger," so the saying goes. Suffering builds character once we can counter the hopelessness with action. Suffering serves as a powerful invitation to build compassion, peace, and liberation from the self. It can be a transformational tool. Harnessing the physiological, physical, and emotional energy of suffering can transform its negative effect on us. Redirecting suffering for inward change blocks its destructive spirit.

Pema Chödrön, a Tibetan Buddhist nun, develops this thought in the practice of Tonglen, the practice of meditating on giving and receiving compassion. She advocates using what seems like poison as medicine. We can use our personal suffering as the path to compassion for all beings.

Jumping from poison to medicine seems like a huge leap. But it's a leap that we can make to convert our suffering into positive growth.

GOD'S INVITATION: PERSEVERANCE

Perseverance is an old-fashioned virtue. Not many people put it in the list of top virtues to strive for today. For me, perseverance conjures the mental image of bundling up in a parka, mittens, boots, and scarf to maintain my balance walking down an icy street in the bitter cold gusts of a Midwest winter! The picture pits me against the whole world of Mother Nature.

Perseverance keeps us on our course of action and purpose in spite of obstacles, difficulties, or discouragement. We gut it out with determination. We build up stamina. We exhibit tenacity. We extend our endurance.

You might be familiar with the nautical expression of the "bitter end." The phrase refers to the end of a mooring rope. The line is as long as it is; there's nothing more. To go on until the bitter end means that the rope is strung out completely from the boat to the dock. With perseverance, the bitter end means that a person will endure the total length of suffering no matter how unpleasant or difficult it is.

Some days, some situations are like that. They require the courage and all the guts we have to walk forward. We muster every ounce of energy just to make it through our daily activities…until we reach our bitter end.

Even Mother Teresa struggled with perseverance. "I know God will never give me anything that I can't handle," she said, "but I wish He didn't trust me so much." Her humor shows that the suffering is conquerable.

We can learn a great deal from each other, so I'm going to share a story of a friend of mine. We can model ourselves after him when faced with any kind of adversity.

My friend Phil is perseverance expert. He has suffered through major challenges: the loss of a son to drugs, the rupture of a lumbar disc 50 years ago that resulted in chronic back pain, a daily morphine pump, type 2 diabetes, and diabetic peripheral neuropathy. Phil knows perseverance!

"I am mentally and physically tough, and persistent. I don't give up. I won't let myself be beaten by others or fate," he says. "I have a great faith and confidence in myself. I bounce back every time. Because of this, I do not fear setbacks anymore."

Phil believes that fear paralyzes people causing inaction. Following Phil's formula for battling adversity, we must toss out fear in favor of perseverance, a stronger attitude. He believes options always exist. If one thing doesn't work, try something else. He advises patience rather than tunnel vision is essential when looking for a solution.

"Start seeking help now," he advises. "Quit sitting in your chair procrastinating and hurting. Networking and taking action, even in the wrong direction, teaches you the right direction and at least gives you the feeling that you are partially in charge of your life. The more you know, the faster you learn."

To aid his perseverance, Phil adheres to one goal: to understand what God has in store for him and to surrender to God's will and plan. "I believe that God is continuously teaching humans how to improve their lives," he explains. "I was put on this earth to improve my soul and to help others. I struggle to overcome my own physical impairments in part to help others who are suffering the same fate. This makes it easier for me to bear up under my own pain."

We can all take a lesson from Phil's playbook. Copying his attitude can help us transform the pain of suffering into a journey of connection.

To start, we need to build the strength for perseverance. Intellectually, we know there is no way around the darkness needed for transformation. But getting our emotional selves to follow is the challenge. We can start with a mnemonic device of what to do in a time of adversity: JUMP. Each of the letters stands for a step to practice.

- **Jump** through whatever hoop is put in front of you, whether that means a frightening doctor's appointment, a painful meeting, or getting started in recovery. Keep focusing on the ultimate goal, so you can celebrate the baby steps in the process. Just like the plodding tortoise that won the race with the hare, never give up on yourself or God.

- **Understand** that there is a Divine Order, the synchronicity of things working out the way they should in the end. We are not privy to the entire picture of our lives and its unfolding. We know that with God, the events will all work out for the best.

- **Meet** every day with a sense of purpose. Reconnect with your destiny. You are here on this earth for a reason. What lessons are you learning? How can you serve others in spite of your pain? You don't have to ace the course; just plow through it as gracefully as possible.

- **Pray** for Divine assistance. Ask for the patience, support, and comfort from God, knowing that all prayers are answered. You may not understand God's ways but never lose your Divine connection.

Practicing JUMP several times a day can provide the first step in building perseverance. The repetition helps convey our attitude to a new place. Instead of wallowing in hopeless suffering, we can take hold of it and use the gift of perseverance to put suffering in its place.

PRAYER

Dear Lord, Sometimes I don't understand your ways and what you are asking of me, but please grant me the strength to transform my suffering into a peaceful surrender.

12

CREATING HOPE

Death does not wait to see if things are done or not done.
—Kularnava

"This time we'll surely have a boy," I pronounced.

Dad had just announced that my Mom was pregnant for the fourth time. What are the odds that she would have four girls in a row? As Mom neared 40 years old, the pressure mounted to produce a long awaited son.

The months flew by with the hustle of a new school year well under way. Lying in bed one chilly night planning my Halloween costume, Dad opened my bedroom door and announced that he needed to take Mom to the hospital to have the baby. As the oldest child, Dad put me in charge of my little sisters.

"What? Not yet!" I blurted out. "The baby is due in January, and this is too early." I wrestled with the timing of it all. A fleeting thought for myself recognized that Mom would be leaving before figuring out our Halloween costumes.

As dawn broke, I couldn't wait for the news. Boy or girl? Scurrying into my parent's bedroom where my dad was fast asleep, I nudged him for the info. Not knowing or caring if he had been up all night at the hospital, I shouted, "Did we have a boy or a girl?"

As Dad rolled over, he mumbled through his grogginess, "We had a girl. And then we had another girl!"

"What do you mean? We had two girls? Mom had twins?"

"There is something wrong with them." He wiped his eyes. Disappointment shaped his face and the edge of fear crept into his voice. "They are six weeks premature, and their lungs are not fully developed. They probably won't make it."

I felt everything collapse: my face, my shoulders, my knees.

My tiny twin sisters died two days later. My mom never did see them. It was just too painful. Her strong German upbringing that shaped her helped her push on. There was no time for grieving with a robust family to care for.

Dad, my two sisters, and I attended the small burial service, but not Mom. The priest said the last rights to send the two angels to heaven. The twins lay side by side in one white satin casket. Julie Ann wore a white nightgown with blue flowers, and Joan Marie mirrored her twin in a white nightgown with pink roses. They nestled closely, like in the womb. Appearing like two painted porcelain dolls, the twins never knew what grief they dealt us.

The whole episode shrouded me in a bad nightmare. Dad, usually the strong head of the household famed for demanding do it my way or the highway, broke into uncontrollable tears in the arms of our neighbors.

Mom—the steadfast reliable person that could handle all emergencies—shuttered herself in their room.

In a matter of days, my world flipped upside down. A week earlier, my family skipped across town looking at new houses. We searched out a bigger home to house our soon-to-be larger family. But so quickly, without warning, the birth and death of the twins shattered us like an earthquake.

CREATING HOPE

Grief weighs heavy on us. Even time fails to heal some grief. We can carry a huge hole in our hearts at the loss of family members or close friends. The sorrow can form deep scars. While the twins were only part of our lives for a couple days, I still think about them. Decades later, I still feel the loss of them.

We all face grief. It's part of the human condition. But in order to avoid losing ourselves to grief, we need to put adversity in its proper perspective. Father Richard Rohr, from the Center for Action and Contemplation, commented in a conference in Phoenix in 2015 that we now know grief is a powerful portal into soul's work and transformation. He explained that grief is a time for waiting in the darkness for wisdom and hope. Grief is an essential part of our development, and the process of moving toward wisdom. Once we take steps towards wisdom, we have hope.

Tragedy allows us to remove all of the false self and ego to move on spiritually with hope. It is the tool that makes us transform into something newer and better. On a simplistic level, think of baking a cake. We need to take separate ingredients to blend the flavors into a wonderful new concoction. We need to break open the egg, melt the butter, and blend the flour. Each takes on new characteristics as it goes through the mixing and baking process. They need to fall apart before they can blend into the new creation. Similarly, we need to fall apart by sinking into grief before we can become a new creature.

Adversity such as grief can refine our personalities. We all joke that enduring hardship makes us better people, if it doesn't kill us first. While overcoming difficulties won't kill us, the process stretches us in new ways.

Two great mystics—St. John of the Cross and Teresa of Avila—grew to relish the dark night of the soul. They understood that God was working with them in the darkness. Both mystics appreciated the power of dissolving into the Divine work in progress.

Let's break the process of overcoming adversity down in another way. Adversity defines who you are. Going through the process of adversity builds character, adding to your desirable qualities. It develops strength. It increases reliability, resilience, and resourcefulness while broadening creative problem solving. Your ability to overcome obstacles then defines who you are. When the chips are down, the true self emerges. Adversity becomes you.

Adversity also becomes you in another sense. It makes you more becoming, more beautiful. Adversity can elevate you into a better listener, an understanding friend, a loyal confidant, or a respected advisor. When you've been to the depths of darkness, compassion grows for others. The warmth in your compassionate eyes is an attractive gift. Others who are hurting will welcome your air of understanding and empathy.

Where's the bottom line? Adversity is necessary to make you real…a real person. The children's book *The Velveteen Rabbit* provides a description of the importance of hardship. The Rabbit asks, "What is real?" The Skin Horse replies, "It's a thing that happens to you." Becoming real doesn't happen all at once. Like the Velveteen Rabbit, by the time that you are real, most of your hair has been loved off, your eyes drop out, you get loose in the joints, and very shabby. But these things don't matter at all, because once you are real, you can't be ugly, except to people who don't understand.

To become real we have to endure the pain. Reading about pain won't make us real. Watching others face adversity won't make us real. We need to walk through the fire of refinement ourselves. We are each called out of the depths of despair into the light of recovery. Some days, we can feel just like the Velveteen Rabbit: worn, tattered, and vulnerable without fur coating. But our appearance doesn't matter. For we are REAL.

Since adversity plays such a vital role in creating who we are, how do we integrate our grief into our daily lives? We can know intellectually that adversity works for our eventual betterment, but in the midst of immense heartache, no good seems apparent. That's when we need to seek God's invitation for hope!

GOD'S INVITATION: HOPE

Hope focuses the expectation of positive outcomes. Hope clears the surrounding darkness as we seek our way. Hope can take the worst of circumstances into optimistic recovery. Like a kaleidoscope that twists multicolored pieces of color into artistic formations, our lives become a piece of art. Hope gives us the reassurance that the jagged segments will come together to form something beautiful.

Without hope, we are lost. A man once related to me his litany of marital woes, financial problems, and health concerns. He found himself on the floor of his kitchen in a fetal position, with a gun to his head. He had no hope.

He survived. (He lived to tell me about it, didn't he?) But during those hopeless moments on the floor, he did not see a way out.

Fighting to keep hope alive is a daily duty, a routine for each day. We must embrace a frame of mind in which we can follow the poetry of Alexander Pope: "Hope springs eternal amid hardship and calamity." By shifting our paradigm to see the Bigger Picture, we can put daily hardship and suffering into perspective. To establish the Bigger Picture, try this writing exercise for one time when you faced adversity in your life:

- Find an 8- x 11-inch piece of paper.
- Turn in it horizontal, and tri-fold the paper.
- Head the three columns: Before, Now, and What I Learned.

You have the framework now. That's the easy part. The hard part is filling in the three columns. Here's how to do it:

- In the Before column, write what occurred before the painful event.

- In the Now column, describe what or where you are now.

- In the What I Learned column, nail down what you gained through this painful experience.

After detailing each of these parts of an adversity event, re-read them. Look for the synchronicity in your own life. Often, the outcome can provide hope. After all, just like the man on the floor with the gun, you survived.

When I struggled through my divorce, I sunk into one of the darkest periods of my life. So let's look at how I would fill out the chart for my divorce.

- Before: Before my divorce, I judged my happiness by pleasing everyone except me. Everybody liked me. I had many friends.

- Now: I follow my own heart to judge my happiness, sometimes upsetting what people expect from me. I don't judge my success by the number of my friends.

- What I learned: True happiness comes from within, not without.

If I look back at my life, I can see how those friends who stuck with me are the true friends. Hope is with my true friends, not the amount of friends.

To develop this process further, you can examine more times of adversity in your life. This provides an effective strategy to see the Bigger Picture. Using this technique of laying adversity out like a storyboard can help you recognize the lessons you learned along the way. Those lessons are what hold hope.

PRAYER

Dear Lord, help me to accept my burdens as opportunities for growth and understanding. I know that you will surround me with your love as I fight to keep hope alive.

Putting Fear and Failure in Their Place

13
GENERATING RESILIENCE

Having high resilience does not mean it doesn't sometimes sting. —Aisha Mirza

As my husband, Joe, and I walked through a store parking lot, an older, dirty sedan approached us ever so slowly. The clunker of a car stuck out amidst newer automobiles lined up in parking stalls. The young scruffy guy driving the rig stopped to address us.

"I'm not asking for money," he leaned out the window.

We listened.

"I'm from Washington State and could use some help." He glanced at the woman sitting next to him. In the back seat, three kids jostled each other.

The scene reminded me of a weeklong in-depth television investigation in San Diego that exposed the life of panhandlers. Caught on film, beggars refused the work offered to them and repeatedly threw generous donations of food in trashcans. The show reported that one street person pulled in $60,000 annually by panhandling from his designated corner.

Perusing the car and its occupants, I walked on toward our vehicle. I refused to be drawn into the intercourse that would lure me deeper into the guilt pit. If I didn't hear the family's story, I could avoid getting emotionally sucked into their sorrows. But guilt flooded me anyway.

I looked back to check out whether his story held veracity, checking the license plate. Joe opened his wallet and handed a bill to the out-of-towner. The man said something I could not hear to Joe. After the exchange, Joe walked toward me shaking his head and muttering to himself.

Joe and I often debated about handing out money to needy people. Joe always gave; I always walked away with guilt. Berating myself in guilt for not being a bit more charitable, I tried to catch Joe's eyes to detect what transpired between them.

"Well, that was a waste," Joe scowled, gathering up what was left of his self-esteem. He explained that he handed the man a five-dollar bill. While he expected some form of a grateful thank you, instead the man admonished him for being so cheap with his handout. "He ranted at me, shaking the bill, 'This is nothing. five bucks won't even buy my kids milk.'"

I wondered what was worse: to feel guilty about walking away or to be chewed out for giving charity, but being cheap? Joe and I both felt like failures.

CREATING RESILIENCE

Due to the experience with the family in the car, fear of failure shaped our reactions the next time we met a panhandler. In the future, Joe would look away from potential opportunity to help out for fear that he might be reprimanded once again. Who would blame him? Who wants to be burnt twice?

Fear can be the most influential and debilitating of emotions. It determines the current of our actions and reactions. Fear of failure, fear of disappointing people, fear of not being accepted, fear of being laughed at, fear of loss, and fear of not being loved are the strongest motivations in making decisions.

When we succumb to those fears, we fail to react to those around us. We enter a state of paralysis. According to Wayne Dyer, a self-help author and motivational speaker, fear binds up our enthusiasm for life, happiness, new experiences, and connectedness. We remain stuck in the status quo. We opt for safety in the present situation, due to our fears. But life begins on the edge of our comfort zones.

We must break away from paralyzing fears. By overcoming hurdles and experiencing success, we gain resilience. Survival breeds resilience, and success breeds more success!

When I was about 7 years old, the swimming pool gave me many opportunities to create resilience. The first one came when my swimming instructor took me to the deep end of the pool for the first time. I thought I was going to die. The dark abyss threatened to swallow me, and the distance across the pool was so far. I glanced at the big pole lifeguards used to rescue incompetent swimmers. I didn't want to be embarrassed when the teacher had to extend the big pole to rescue me.

Fear kept me stalling as long as possible on the deck, but I finally slid into the pool when my instructor urged me to get in the water. I clung to the pool's rim. Gulping for air, I battled irrational fears from threatening to drown me. When my instructor glared, I pushed off, paddling like crazy. I kicked hard to keep from getting sucked into the abyss, and I swung my arms fast to reach the other side. My hand slapped the pool rim's hard surface. I made it…I lived through the deep end. The deep-end swim was my first step in breaking through my fear to create resilience.

My second paralysis from fear came when on the high dive for the first time. With my feet glued to the back end of the diving board, I stared at the narrow sliver of board and its height off the water. A lack of rails spelled sheer doom in falling off before reaching the springboard's end, and I could hear my friends calling out "baby" or "scaredy cat" if I had to retreat down the steps to the deck.

After inching my way to the end, the water seemed so far away. People jumped off bridges into rivers and died. How is this any different? Would the water smack me when I hit it? Summoning what courage I could find, I finally leapt. Chalk up another success after hurdling the fears.

Life is full of deep ends and high dives. Surviving them teaches us resilience. We can protect our self-esteem in our comfort zones by succumbing to our fears, or we can take a leap into the deep end or off the high dive. In doing so, we will learn resilience.

GOD'S INVITATION: RESILIENCE

Resilience is like the inflatable children's toy that is designed when knocked down to spring right back up. It is the ability to recover from difficulties. Similar to elasticity, resilience is the quality of being able to bend but not break.

While resilience is an admirable goal to weather attacks on our self-esteem, it does not aid us in avoiding trauma, adversity, and setbacks. Hardships still befall us. But resilience allows us to view situations accurately and maintain a cool head with well-grounded decision-making abilities while the storm whirls around us.

To build resilience requires key attitudes: maintaining a positive mentality, managing emotions, and believing in our own abilities. Throw victim mentality out the door as it inhibits developing resilience.

How do we build the ability to rebound from the disappointments and failures that life hands us? Guided imagery can help. Repeating a short, guided mediation can build a positive self-belief system and broaden optimistic attitudes. When wrestling with fear of failure or fear of disappointing others, try these steps:

STEP 1: GAINING PROTECTION

This step uses bright light. Use sun, star, or bulb light, whichever works for you.

- Imagine a bright white light several feet above your head. Make it bright enough to be blinded by the force of its strength if your eyes were open.

- Envision rays shooting out from the light, radiant and glowing.

- Lengthen the streaks of light to shine down on you with them caressing every inch of your body. See them cover your entire being until you are bathed with a white light.

The white light is a shield to protect you from all negative energy. This light is strong. Nothing can stain or penetrate it. It is your protective layer of strength. It will fend off all guilt and comments that others may hurl at you. Your magical coating of light acts like Teflon. Nothing clings to it. It repels all hurt, sadness, or regret. You are safe beneath the white light.

Once you have mastered envisioning the white light surrounding you, then you can tackle the second step. It's time to practice imagining arrows failing to penetrate your light.

STEP 2: FENDING OFF ARROWS

With your internal eye, it's time to watch hurtful judgments, expectations of others, and criticism slide off your light. Imagine them as arrows, rocks, or buckets of liquid hurling toward you, but hitting the light and falling down to the ground. They are unable to penetrate your light shield, and feelings of unworthiness will not take hold.

- Visualize harsh words of unfair criticism dropping off your protective coating.

- See guilt thrown your way boomeranging back away from you.

- Watch cruel judgments deflate into thin air.
- Look for disappointment from others slipping into oblivion.

Keep breathing as you practice visualizing your light repelling all incoming negativity. Relax knowing that you will not absorb any of the emotional detritus directed at you. No dissatisfaction can get through to you.

You have become a radiant being of light, beaming in all directions. You are safe behind your white light. By practicing this guided imagery, following your own heart will be easier for you. When you have to say "no" to protect your own happiness, you will no longer fear the reaction of others. Your magical coat keeps their responses at bay, and your light sustains your joy.

This two-step guided imagery can help build resilience. As in any guided imagery, you may need to repeat its practice over and over for it to take hold. By imagining yourself bathed in protective light that is capable of shunning all negativity, you can begin to build resilience.

Practice this guided imagery three times a day to start. Then add another quick session any time you feel negativity coming toward you.

PRAYER

Dear Lord, I know that I'm here to learn through failure, disappointments, and setbacks. Surrounded by your strength and penetrating light, I will be able to cope with any problem feeling your constant love and support.

14
CALLING FORTH FORGIVENESS

The truth is, unless you let go, unless you forgive yourself, unless you forgive the situation, unless you realize that the situation is over, you cannot move forward.
—Steve Maraboli

As I grasped my preview copy of *A Change of Habit* for the first time, the joy of accomplishment flooded over me. Nearly five years of writing, editing, and rewriting went into the project. Much of the challenge came from searching for the exact words to describe my spiritual journey from being a Catholic nun known as Sister Mary Kateri to life outside the convent as Sister Mary Vodka. I wanted to share my religious trek in hope that my experiences would help other people protect their own relationship with God.

Eager to bring my family into the celebration, I sent each sibling a copy of the book. I also took the files to the print shop to have the manuscript reproduced in 18-point type so my nearly blind mother could enjoy the book without eyestrain.

Weeks following my book gift, I awaited the kudos from my family. They came from my siblings, but my mother lagged in responding. Finally, I could wait no longer for her maternal blessing.

"How did you like the book, Mom?"

"Well, Pat," she hesitated, "the book is okay, but I have one request. Could you take your maiden name off that cover?"

My heart sank. Instead of Patty Ptak Kogutek, my mother insisted on Patty Kogutek. Disappointment coursed through me. Then my stomach tightened with anger. How could my very own mother fail to appreciate my journey, some of which involved my various names?

"Why do you want me to take my name off the book?" I demanded.

"Oh, honey, this book embarrasses you. It's an embarrassment to our family. The nuns certainly won't approve of it, and the Catholic Church won't like it."

Blindsided by her disparagement, I stammered a semblance of a response about how proud the book made me feel. I assured her that I tried my best not to offend anyone in the recounting of my story. She needed to understand that the book was my story and that journey of growth reflected in my eight different names: Patty Ptak, Sister Mary Kateri, Sister Mary Patricia, Patty Ptak, Patty Kimer, Patty Ptak, Patty Kogutek and Dr. Patty Kogutek. Matter of fact, the name Ptak was the one constant repeat!

EMPLOYING FORGIVENESS

I had no intention of removing my middle name off the cover of the book, despite my mother's demand. But I wondered if I could ever get beyond my mother's lack of support. As her lack of caring and understanding slighted me, my disappointment blossomed from anger to the loneliness of rejection.

In writing my book, I spilled my emotions on the page. I dug deep into scars for details. I hoped that readers would have compassion for my struggle with guilt. But the only person missing compassion was Mom.

Replaying her objections over and over in my head, I envisioned erecting a wall between the two of us. I complained about Mom to anyone that would listen. My anger mushroomed. One day, threatened with losing myself to the anger, I set it aside.

In the pause, I took another look at Mom. In thinking over her role in my story, I pieced together the fabric of her hostility toward my book. Mom felt guilt. She had the same guilt that I wrote about in the book.

She felt guilt for failing to help me when I was so lonely in the convent. When I visited my family in California during my first summer in the convent, I sought a semblance of my old life and the family I knew. But Mom had thrown away all my clothes and treasures, including my beloved music albums and high school yearbooks. Her disregard for my personal belongings crushed me. Her excuse that she thought I did not have a need for them any longer in the convent drove me further into depression.

But when I looked at my story from Mom's point of view, I realized that she felt guilt at the unhappiness disclosed in my memoir. She felt guilty for throwing out my things. She felt guilty for not recognizing how unhappy I was in the convent. She felt guilty for letting her daughter suffer.

I adjusted my viewpoint to let the doors of conversation open up for us. Mom confessed that she was angry with me for leaving the family. I gave her a pass for throwing my personal things out. After all, most moms would discard unnecessary baggage to move a family of five from Nebraska to California.

I reaffirmed her motherly skills by removing her guilt for failing to rescue me from the convent. With every letter censored to ensure only happiness leaked out of the hallowed convent walls, she was not responsible for knowing what I felt.

I forgave her. She forgave me. Communication between us resumed. The next time I saw her in her retirement home, she wheeled her walker down the hall, as she held my book up high for admiration from everyone she met along the way.

"Does anyone want to read OUR book?" she offered to her fellow residents. She held the book up—even with my maiden name on the cover.

For Mom and I to reach forgiveness, we had to give up blaming each other. She had to quit blaming me for abandoning the family, and I had to cease blaming her for throwing out my childhood possessions.

Blaming others prevents us from moving on into forgiveness. But some people do not like to accept responsibility for their own actions. They have an excuse for everything that does not go their way. They blame everyone else for their unpleasant situations. If they listened to themselves, they would be astonished to hear how many times a day they blame their unhappiness on others.

It is so easy to fall into the blaming pit, justifying our choices, decisions, and actions. But how do we move past our hurt to accepting responsibility for our own happiness?

GOD'S INVITATION: FORGIVENESS

Forgiveness may be the biggest of God's invitations to us. Being part of the human family, we so easily encounter injustices, damaged feelings, and hurt. Forgiveness is the conscious choice to release resentment. It grants pardon. It is the decision to offer absolution to people who have harmed us, whether they deserve it or not.

Herein is the stumbling block: Many times we are justified in our anger. Our resentment may be valid, and others who have treated us poorly may deserve our hostility. Those who have abused us or treated us maliciously warrant the lack of affection from us. Those who have transgressed the law against us truly justify our anger. We hang on to our negative emotions because, damn it, they deserve it!

But forgiveness is not about condoning misbehavior. It does not forget inappropriate behavior. It does not excuse wrongdoing.

Instead, forgiveness is for us, the recipients—the ones experiencing the hurt, the torment, and the pain. Power comes from forgiveness when we experience the release of negativity. Forgiveness frees us to no longer be bound by our own energy draining anger.

When we forgive, we choose to let go of the

negative force that creates the pain in our hearts. We cannot control the actions of others, but we can control our attitudes. Sometimes that's the only choice we have. We can choose to move forward with the invitation of forgiveness.

One way to move into forgiveness is to examine the blaming. To see how utterly ridiculous blaming can become, experiment with two awareness techniques in the Blame Game.

Start by playing the first part of the Blame Game. This game blatantly shifts all responsibility to others in every situation. Almost to the point of ridiculous. List out your negative emotions and who or what causes each one of them. List out what you can't do because of other people or things. Go into the minute emotions. Take a look at my list with my mom:

- I felt slighted when Mom threw out my childhood treasures while I was in the convent.

- My choice to enter the convent did not deserve the loss of my treasures.

- Mom's throwing out my childhood treasures deserves 40 years of holding a grudge.

Oftentimes, it's funny to see how far we go to avoid accepting responsibility. When we look at my last statement, it's obvious how ridiculous my grudge was. You can discover some of yours this way.

The second part of the Blame Game is to catch and count. This requires stopping yourself when you attempt to make excuses during your day. You must develop an eye for shifting the responsibility. Count the number of times per day that you spend blaming others, justifying your actions, or making excuses for the way things are. Consider the number of minutes and hours wasted on wallowing in blame rather than moving forward. If you can elevate your awareness of the amount of time devoted to blaming, it becomes easier to change this damaging behavior.

If you see a pattern of sidestepping an issue or a certain person, that may be time to look at forgiveness. Look at what is behind the blaming and seek elements that you can forgive.

Forgiveness begins within. It begins with forgiving ourselves for past mistakes and human failures. Once we accept responsibility for our own actions and forgive ourselves, we can radiate this understanding outward to others. We can forgive others for their human failings in dealing with us. This brings us the freedom to move beyond.

Once we allow ourselves the freedom to move beyond blaming others, we will experience the true nature of forgiveness. That is the best gift of an all-loving God.

PRAYER

Dear Lord, You understand our human nature, our hurt feelings, and past failings. Please help me to accept my own foibles, let go of the pain caused by others, and experience your true peace of mind.

15 PROMOTING CONFIDENCE

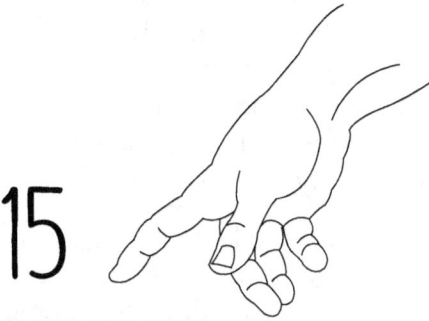

Go confidently in the direction of your dreams.
—Henry David Thoreau

When my husband, Joe, and I visited Sedona, Arizona, we kept our eyes open for evidence that it was appropriately known as the vortex of spirituality. We sat in the shadows of the russet mountains enjoying an al fresco lunch as the bright sun climbed overhead. I sipped my prickly pear margarita. Being the spiritual seeker that I am, I sat ready for Divine contact, a spiritual message.

As I savored a spicy enchilada, I noticed a beautiful woman with a lock of gray hair fashionably pulled on top of her head and secured with a bright pink flower. That flower matched her pink and purple outfit with color-coordinated pink shoes. "The years had been good to her, sans makeup," I mused, assessing her to be in her late 70s.

She sat alone soaking up the red mountain beauty. The glorious mountains almost paled in comparison to this woman's spectrum of color. She reminded me of a bright flower that lived according to the adage "Bloom where you are planted."

Mesmerized by this strange bright-hued woman, I stared. She nonchalantly sipped her soup and slathered her burger with mayonnaise. She seemed comfortable with herself and her aloneness. I sensed a woman of wisdom. Intuitively, I knew she had an important spiritual message for me.

As she gathered her belongings to exit, I gave her one of my biggest smiles to draw her over to our table. As she approached our table, I complimented her on her choice of clothing being so full of life and happy, like a kaleidoscope.

Her eyes twinkled, and a broad smile grew across her face. "At my age," she explained, "I can be a trendsetter rather than a follower."

She knew she beaconed like a trendsetter. Confidence beamed from her as she strode out. I wondered if she always had been a trendsetter or if that came later on with the wisdom of age. Either way, she demonstrated how to be comfortable with one's self. I smiled, recognizing that I shouldn't wait to be her age to be who I was.

DEVELOPING CONFIDENCE

Why do we feel that we have to wait until we age to be who we are meant to be? We spend our precious time living as chameleons, changing our colors to please others. Sometimes, our real selves are buried deep within, waiting for the right time when it's safe to let people know what and who we truly are.

We fear being who we really are. We are fearful of standing out too far from the accepted crowd. We don't want to ruffle feathers, speak our truth, or stand on the wrong side of the popular issues. We fear being shunned for who we are.

Respecting yourself and who you are on your own journey can cause a few missteps along the way. Sadly, in my first marriage, I couldn't speak my truth until the end of the relationship.

My husband loved to water ski. To my dismay, we could not fit a washer and dryer in the garage because the ski boat was so long. Fitting in diagonally, it precluded parking our cars in the garage, too.

Every weekend before sunrise, we packed up the boat to head to our special beach to catch the calm water at daybreak for water skiing. We spent the whole day cutting through the wake, jumping over the rising crest, and pulling our friends around in circles. This weekend ritual went on for years, during which I dreaded trudging to the Laundromat every week.

One week, I watched the clothes spinning in the dryer. "You could have your own washer and dryer, but NO!" I muttered to myself. "We have to make room for our treasured boat." I scowled and then brushed the negative thought from my head. A washer and dryer wouldn't please my husband as much as the boat, and our friends depended on our boat for water skiing.

After my marriage broke up, I felt the freedom to become who I was meant to be and participate in the sports that I enjoyed. To my surprise, I discovered that I really didn't enjoy water skiing. The water was too cold. I hated getting up so early on weekends. I loathed having to make room for the boat in my garage, especially at the expense of a washer and dryer.

I had to face a lot of pent up anger about our boat. But it represented the way I behaved in my marriage. I disrespected my own wants, needs, and desires in favor of pleasing my husband. I played the good sport, agreeing with what others wanted; I went along with the popular decision. My fear of not fitting in with our group of water ski friends drove me further down the road of denial. Surely, voicing my dissenting opinion would cause a tremendous ripple or lead to a devastating tsunami.

But so often what we fear is not as huge as we construe it to be. "I quit being afraid when my first venture failed and the sky didn't fall down," said Allen H. Neuharth, founder of *USA Today*. Often when we show who we really are, other people accept us despite our fears. Even if they don't, the sky does not fall down.

As my friend, Gail Larsen advises, "Be yourself, everyone else is already taken." We must have confidence to do that.

GOD'S INVITATION: CONFIDENCE

Confidence acts as a supporting beam in building our life's work. Confidence is that belief that you can count on some thing or someone, in this case, our selves.

In the *Sihera Confidence Guide*, the "Confidence Triangle" is described as consisting of three elements: a level of achievement, a sense of belonging, and life acceptance. These three elements interact to give us our vital self-esteem.

- A **sense of belonging** grows from the day we were born. This sense of belonging is a basic need of both mind and soul. From childhood, this sense of connectedness and association grows or diminishes with our interactions with friends and family. Our relationships with others build our feeling of being welcomed or unwelcomed, valued or unvalued, wanted or unwanted.

- A **level of achievement** builds our worthiness. When we meet goals, measuring up to expectations and accepted standards, we increase our own value. Our lives take on new meaning when we see the merit of our actions. We can judge objectively our self-worth.

- **Life acceptance builds self-esteem** culminating in accepting the big picture of our journey. We celebrate the successes and understand that the missteps are stepping-stones to learning and future opportunity. We accept life the way it is, celebrating our happiness within context.

We learn these elements of confidence day in and day out along our journey. These three elements are neither inherited from our parents, nor bought at the store. They are learned, earned, and paid for with our time and energy. Our happiness is dependent upon the emotional health of confidence.

To build confidence, let's use Louise Hay's mirror activity to grow the three elements of confidence: level of achievement, sense of belonging, and level of self esteem.

Place mirrors in various rooms of the house in strategic positions. Louise keeps one by her desk. Friends think that she has it there to check her makeup, but that is not the case. Louse winks and smiles at herself often. She will look right into her own eyes uttering, "I love you, Louise!" She affirms her abilities and self-worth to herself to build confidence.

Most of us are uncomfortable looking at ourselves in the mirror, honing in on the wrinkles, the sagging neck, the hair askew, the extra pounds, and the smudged makeup. But we need to put that behind us and take a loving look at ourselves while stating confidence-boosting affirmations. Affirmations should address things we are doing, rather than our appearance. Here's the self-talk I have practiced for each of the steps:

- **Level of achievement:** "Wow, Patty, this is a great chapter you are writing. Remember the blog post you wrote about this? The readers got some really great ideas and loved it."

- **Sense of belonging:** "Patty, you have lots of wonderful friends who are willing to help at any time. Don't be afraid to ask."

- **Building self-esteem:** "You are the world's best putter. Remember that putt you sank on hole number 9? You can do it again, anytime.

After working with the mirror exercises and affirmations, you will become your own source of strength. You can walk a little taller, speak up, and carry yourself with pride.

What others think of you will not carry the weight that it once did. You will take on an air of confidence in yourself, your mission, and your abilities.

PRAYER

Dear Lord, Please help me to come to know and love the wonderful me that you created. You have given me a special purpose on this earth, and I have confidence in the gifts, talents, and abilities to accomplish my destiny.

Ditching The Burden Of Guilt

16
STRENGTHENING COURAGE

Negative emotions like loneliness, envy, and guilt have an important role to play in a happy life; they're big, flashing signs that something needs to change.
—Gretchen Rubin

"A Marian girl is in the right place, doing the right thing, at the right time," I recited the words from our Marian High School handbook. I recalled the expectation appearing in print and this motto of perfection echoing after being dictated by our nuns. The motto aided in grooming us to be future Stepford Wives, clones of perfection.

As I packed my suitcase for our 50th high school reunion, the motto of perfection remained etched vividly in my brain. Marian High School operated as a small all-girls Catholic high school in Omaha, Nebraska. Four hundred students attended Marian in the early 1960s, and our graduating class touted 88 girls on the cutting edge of the baby boom.

Our nuns, dressed in floor-length black and white habits, prided themselves on pushing advanced education and producing well-behaved young ladies. They enforced rules of dress, prim behavior, and high expectations. They left little room for choices. We were taught what to wear, what movies to watch, what to think, what to read, and how to pray. I followed the nun's rules even when they made no sense to me. It was easier to follow the rules than to pay for misbehavior if caught chewing gum, wearing a skirt that was too short, or not covering my head with a chapel veil.

I took this special reunion weekend to do some personal reflection. Desiring to be the perfect Marian girl was a personal goal of mine. I adopted this motto of perfection: to be in the right place, to do the right thing, and to do both at the right time. I had to be right. With that desire for perfection came a series of shoulds. I should be doing this because it is the right thing to do. I should be there, because that's what's expected. I should, I should, I should.

Marian's high standard of perfection left me replaying the same tape in my mind of having to do everything the right way. Frank Sinatra's song, "I Did It My Way," was the opposite from the theme song for my life: I did it THEIR way. My small world seemed clear. Black or white. Right or wrong. Doing wrong was punishable in my immediate life by confession or in my afterlife by burning in hell. I opted for acting right.

Years later, I've come to understand that there is more than one right answer, more than one right way, and more than one right anything. Rather than black or white, some things can be gray. Rather than right or wrong, some things may be both or neither. In fact, there could be 50 shades of gray.

I've also come to realize that in some ways life comes to us, gently leading us where we should be. Rather than adhering to the rules in the handbook, I needed to focus on my guiding source within. But that takes courage. I know that I am divinely guarded, guided, and gifted. But trusting my inner counselor requires courage.

Celebrating my 50th high school reunion with other alumni brought laughter at memories. But for me, the event served as a measuring stick to see how far I'd come from the Marian girl perfection and reminded me that calling on courage is a daily task to listen to myself.

BUILDING COURAGE

Rereading our school handbook gave me an a-ha moment. In our school's motto, I saw the roots of my striving to be the perfect good girl. For me, trying to be perfect led to a lifetime of behaviors spurred on by guilt.

People shy away from talking about guilt. We don't want to think that we did anything wrong, or that we have any behavior that would cause us to feel guilty. But guilt is a silent, slippery factor causing havoc that influences our decision-making process. The negative effects of guilt are devastating to our health, emotionally, physically, and mentally.

Emotionally, the guilt to be perfect causes a loss of confidence, depression, alienation, apprehension, and irritability. Physically, guilt at trying to be perfect can cause headaches, muscular twitches, fatigue, and shortness of breath. Mentally, the guilt to be perfect wraps us up in worry, indecision, negativity, and poor decision-making skills. These cumulative stresses can rear their ugly heads in loss of appetite, drinking more alcohol, insomnia, and eating disorders.

Guilt works with a long arm to tear apart our health and happiness. Let's look at how the five Ps work to create guilt. Meet the five Ps: Perfecting, Pleasing, Pretending, Performing, and Procrastinating.

- **Perfecting:** For me, failure had never been an option—in school, home, or society. Because our culture scorns failure, we strive to be perfect. Our culture is based on competition, not cooperation, so in our struggle to be perfect, we stand alone without others to assist us. We must be the victor to get the spoils; we must be the fittest in order to survive. Those attitudes include one person—the perfect winner—rather than multiple people who assist each other. With that singularity in competition, one must rise to perfection alone. Failing perfection means being a loser, and no one admires a loser.

- **Pleasing:** Because we want people to like us, we aim to please. Pleasing parents, teachers, authority figures, and friends ensures their happiness, and our daily world runs smoothly with no upsets to the status quo. Failing to please makes others show displeasure toward us; it also introduces anger, disruption, and discordance into our lives.

Perfecting and pleasing are two of the most common forces behind decision-making. We make decisions in order to be perfect and please others. Motivated by these forces, we engage in guilt avoidance behaviors. These are three more Ps.

- **Pretending:** To avoid the guilt, we pretend circumstances are different than they really are. Ditching all personal honesty, we live in denial.

- **Procrastinating:** To avoid the guilt, we procrastinate. We put off facing the difficult situation. We fool ourselves into thinking a better time will come to handle this hardship.

- **Performing:** To avoid the guilt, we perform. We go through the motions without really feeling what we are doing. We meet everyone's expectations, putting our own desires and needs on hold. Devoid of any real passion, we fulfill responsibilities like robots.

Living our lives with the five Ps leads to a situation that damages our freedom and happiness. By Perfecting, Pleasing, Pretending, Performing, and Procrastinating, we erect the bars ourselves of our own prisons. We create our very own Personal Prisons.

What does it take to leave these Ps behind? We need courage to Protect and Promote our own happiness.

GOD'S INVITATION: COURAGE

To break out of our personal prisons may be a relearning process for many. Some people have been conditioned from childhood to follow instructions and obey. Stepping away from the rules and expectations can be scary. It can threaten our very core. Being willing to disappoint others and live with failure takes courage.

Courage is stronger than fear. But courage does not take away the fear. Mark Twain commented that, "Courage is not the absence of fear. It is acting in spite of it."

When we think of courage we may envision a knight dressed in armor, prepared to slay the dragon beast. The knight is willing to put his life on the line for a bigger cause—to save others suffering at the hands of the dragon.

Courage in our daily lives means that we must find the strength to speak our truths. We need to follow the tugs in our hearts, boldly following our own purpose. We need to slay the dragons of pleasing and perfecting.

In order to slay the dragons, we need to be our own superheroes. There can be certain trigger words or trigger people that evoke conforming actions from us. When a parent, teacher, or an authority figure speaks of what you should, ought, or must do, the status of the speaker adds such weight to their suggestion that it becomes a command. In our old ways of pleasing and perfecting, we behave exactly as suggested. Confronting the beasts takes more than our usual perfecting and pleasing responses.

To become your own superhero requires a metamorphosis. It includes a physical and mental conversion. Practice these two visualizations:

- Physically, make yourself larger, able bodied, and stronger. Pull your neck tall like a giraffe, throw you shoulders back, and puff yourself up with a deep breath. Visualize a complete transfiguration. This is the bigger, stronger, bolder you.

- Mentally, imagine yourself surrounded by an army of angels. These mighty creatures act a protective shield for all injuries, injustices, and inhospitalities that might come your way.

These are the visions to summon when you need courage. Physically and mentally, these visualizations make you ready for whatever comes your way. They help protect your own happiness. You may fail, and you may disappoint, but you are ready to handle it. You are the knight surrounded by angels. You are no longer a lone warrior, but part of an army.

Courage does not prevent facing the challenge. Courage demands facing the challenge and continuing to deal with the repercussions of your actions. In the past, people have always counted on you to behave in a certain way. They always rely on you for conforming to their wishes. When you cross that line, disappointing them, be ready for a cold shoulder or a verbal confrontation.

Mustering up ourselves as superheroes gives us courage. With that courage, we can throw out the five Ps to be who we are and follow our own destiny.

PRAYER

Dear Lord, you put me on this earth for a particular reason. Help me to find the courage to be who I'm called to be, speaking the truth from my heart, fulfilling my destiny.

17

MAINTAINING SANITY

The statistics on sanity are that one out of every four Americans is suffering from some form of mental illness. Think of your three best friends. If they're okay, then it's you. —Rita Mae Brown

Guilt pops up when I least expect it. It attacks me in the most insipid ways.

When I pulled in the parking lot, the sign at the shopping center read "Customer Parking Only." I slid my car into a stall. But my appointment was in the office around the corner from the shopping center. Then, I bit my lip in guilt. My business was not in the shopping center; hence, I was not a customer and not qualified for customer parking only. Wanting to ease my guilty conscience, I came up with the only lawful solution: to become a customer.

I dipped into the beauty supply shop and bought three unnecessary products. I figured, if one item was good, then three purchases ought to really qualify me for my parking space. I breathed a sigh of relief at fulfilling the letter of the law. Leaving my car in the lot, I hurried off to my scheduled appointment. My irrational answer to my parking helped me intellectually say I was guilt-free, but inside guilt still tweaked at me.

Guilt has its own way of following me throughout the day, no matter where I am. It even shows up in my kitchen when I'm preparing a home-cooked meal.

My recipe called for a teaspoon of crushed garlic. I huffed at the unpleasant process of first fighting with the small clove to peel it followed by the tricky hand maneuver of fitting it into the press for crushing. I opened the refrigerator in search of a jar of prepared crushed garlic. Instead of garlic scenting my fingers, I could cheat by opening the jar and simply spooning out a teaspoon.

Guilt shot through me as I drew the jar from the fridge. I remembered reading recipes in *Bon Appetite*. The magazine never once instructed readers to open a jar of garlic. After all, good cooks went for fresh ingredients.

I wrestled with myself. Since I wanted to cook the best for my family, I should not settle for the jarred garlic with half the taste of the real hand-pressed flavor. My acclaimed recipe deserved the real zing of fresh garlic, and giving my best effort ought to mean peeling the cloves by hand. Besides, would anyone know that I cheated with jarred garlic?

"Guilt, be damned!" I proclaimed, twisting the lid off the jar of garlic. I inhaled the pungent odor and reached for a teaspoon. "No one will ever know!" Despite my choice, guilt at using jarred garlic niggled me for the next hour.

MAINTAINING SANITY

Oh, the crazy mind of a guilt sponge! Guilt is an emotional self-judgment that we inflict on ourselves when not meeting expectations. We set some expectations for ourselves; others set expectations for us.

Guilt is like electricity. A little electricity is a good thing. It can warm food and heat a home. But too much out-of-control electricity can kill a person. It's the same with guilt. A little guilt can keep us on the honest road of integrity, enforcing a moral code with our consciences. But too much guilt can bring us to a standstill, afraid to make any decision at all.

Too much self-imagined guilt can create analysis paralysis. We over think things. We linger on every possible fear, afraid to make a move forward. We argue with ourselves. We wonder if we did the right thing or think that we should have done something differently. We may take 45 minutes to make a decision, but then we spend the whole night tossing and turning wondering if we made the right decision. No wonder guilt sponges like me feel perched on the edge of insanity.

Externally created guilt results from expectations from other people. We absorb it from an early age from our families, our upbringing, our culture, and our religion. Let's look at how these work:

- **Families:** Families shape norms for our behavior, our language, and our dress. Acceptable standards are drilled into us at an early age, and parents reinforce moral, cultural, and church expectations, defining what is acceptable and what is right and wrong. "When you are in my house, you will follow our rules" is the parental dictum. Obedience from us makes for smooth sailing. But parents also feel guilt. In a recent publication, one mother shared, "I feel guilty all the time because I can't be everywhere at once. I feel like I want to be there for everybody, whoever needs me. I just worry about them all." Guilt forces children and parents to maintain family expectations.

- **Upbringing:** Birth order can also have an effect on guilt. First-born children may have responsibilities for younger siblings. They are also held up as role models. Guilt keeps first-born children shouldering the burden for helping both parents and younger siblings.

- **Culture:** We are also saturated with a culture imposing more expectations. The mores of society dictate our behavior, especially with strong expectations of the sexes. Despite the changing role of women in culture since World War II, women are still expected to be the caregivers, demure and soft. If a woman in the workplace exhibits strong masculine qualities, she is deemed a hard ass or bitch. Men, on the other hand, are expected to be the breadwinners, protectors, strong, and unyielding with little room for sensitivity to emotions. Told to "Man up," men are denounced as babies if they exhibit their softer side. Guilt keeps us behaving in ways that reinforce outmoded definitions of the sexes.

- **Religion:** The authority found in formal religions is strong, teaching rules of behavior based on beliefs and reinforced through rites and rituals. Authority works as a hierarchy...top down. Rules funnel down to be obeyed. Fear and guilt keep the faithful in line.

Guilt bombards us. It comes from our families, upbringing, culture, and religion. No wonder guilt sponges like me struggle to maintain our sanity under the colossal weight that it carries. Since guilt won't disappear entirely, we must find a way to manage it in order to remain sane.

GOD'S INVITATION: SANITY

Sanity reflects a reasonableness and healthy sound judgment. In legal terms, sanity is defined as whether a person was in complete control of their mental faculties at a particular time. My two incidences, in the parking lot and the kitchen, reflect a mind hijacked by guilt. I lost my reasonableness and sound judgment. My mental powers of evaluating normal every day situations were diminished by the pressures of having to follow the rules, the letter of the law, no matter what made sense.

Allowed to mushroom, guilt builds a rickety foundation of constant worry. This perennial state of guilt is a form of insanity, as plagues of guilt take us out of our right minds. We need to take protective control of our thoughts to manage our sanity. We need to reign over our mental judgments by controlling our thoughts. Doubt, worry and guilt will still exist, but we don't have to devote so many hours to them. Worry should not be at the center of each decision we make.

We need to teach ourselves how to put guilt in its rightful place. I suggest scheduling a certain time of the day to address the worries that come from guilt. Specify a Worry Time: early in the morning, for 20 minutes after lunch, or in late afternoon after the guilt of the day builds up. Set aside a designated time when you are relaxed, quiet, and serene. Then, you can address the worries in a sane manner. Being relaxed puts you in control of your thoughts. You can determine your actions in a logical way rather than merely reacting to guilty feelings. Avoid setting Worry Time at bedtime as you don't want to go to sleep in that state.

Setting a specific **Worry Time** lets you dismiss the cumbersome load of guilt when you encounter it in your day. You can defer dealing with it until a later time. When a bothersome guilt thought enters your mind, mentally put it in a **Worry Vault** to be dealt with at the appointed time. This vault guards these haunting thoughts, keeping them at bay and you in a saner place. Placing that guilt thought in the Worry Vault will allow you to move past ruminating in a circular argument of what you should or should not do.

Then, at the designated Worry Time, unlock the Worry Vault. Examine only one worry at a time, listening to yourself and determining what you want to do. Avoid giving credence to all the shoulds and oughts from other people. Control your thoughts by making full sentence statements rather than posing unanswerable questions. After making a decision on one worry, you can move on to the next one. When Worry Time is up, quit. Leave the remaining guilt in the Worry Vault for your next session. Breathe deeply, and go about your day.

When it comes to controlling guilt, maintaining a sense of sanity is imperative. Putting guilt in its place will allow you to control your thoughts, your life, and your happiness.

PRAYER

Dear Lord, worry and guilt sometimes plague my peace, pulling me away from your joy. Help me to maintain a healthy mind, making sound decisions ensuring my ability to serve you wisely.

18

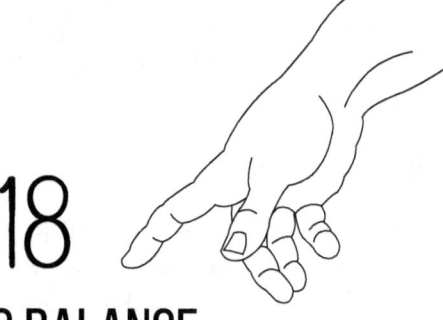

SUSTAINING BALANCE

My point is, life is about balance. The good and the bad. The highs and the lows. The pina and the colada.
—Ellen DeGeneres, *Seriously…I'm Kidding*

Plucking a thong from the laundry basket, I tried to fold it. First, one way, and then the other. My anal-retentive genes compelled me to fold the miniscule fabric. But in frustration, I succumbed to impatience and tossed the undies on top of the folded stack of lingerie.

With my laundry project complete, I collapsed to rest on the den sofa. My back and feet both complained at once, and I groaned in response. Then, I lolled my head back with a sigh. The couch felt so good.

Glancing at the coffee table for some mindless reading material, I selected a fashion magazine. The colorful fashions mesmerized me, and an article updated me on what's in and what's out. My body began to relax. I sank into the sofa while my breathing took on a languid tempo.

The sound of the garage door opening intruded on my reverie. The electric door chain clanged, and the motor whirred. I went into alert: Joe's home!

Tossing all rational thinking aside, I jumped up and grabbed the stacks of folded laundry. I didn't want Joe to see me sitting down. Doing nothing. I didn't want to appear lazy. So I busied myself with rearranging the stacks of folded laundry on the coffee table.

A vision of my mother, my female role model, surfaced from my memory. Mom, mother of five children, never had a moment's rest. I never saw her sitting down to rest. She never had the luxury of any frivolous activity such as reading a magazine. She performed her role as a constant caregiver—cooking, washing, housecleaning, and tending to the needs of her family.

Images of the nuns in high school followed. They flitted through my head along with their admonishing words, "An idle mind is the devil's workshop."

At home and at school, keeping busy was held in high esteem. Idleness produced laziness. Perhaps staying active kept us out of trouble, so we always strove to appear productive. Whatever the motivation, busy-ness ranked up there with sainthood.

As Joe entered the house, I fiddled with the laundry stacks. When he walked in the den to greet me, he saw the folded laundry as a sign of a productive afternoon. The stacks perched neatly on the coffee table as some sort of activity award, and I beamed with my accomplishment. After marching the stacks of laundry into the bedroom to put away, I strode to the kitchen where I clanged pots and pans. I felt compelled to appear organized for the next activity—dinner preparation. Compulsion to appear busy was paramount.

SEEKING BALANCE

Even though Joe would not have condemned me for lounging on the couch reading a magazine, my upbringing reinforced a pattern of behavior that forbade me from appearing with any semblance of laziness. This silly episode resounds with the admonition that many of us grew up with: Make yourself useful; don't just sit there like a bump on a log. Society values productive activity. Physical accomplishments can be observed, judged, and measured, and checking items off our to-do lists bring pride.

We over schedule our calendars. We cram our days with assignments, appointments, and meetings. A full calendar bolsters our self-esteem. We judge our importance and self-worth by how many people depend on us, how much we do, how much we can give, and how our time was well invested. Cell phones and the Internet feed our need to be occupied. We always have communications to catch up on with emails, texting, and Facebook. We glorify being occupied.

But investing so much importance in busy-ness can lead to an unhealthy lifestyle. It can even be destructive. We can lose ourselves in activity. When we do, we dismiss time needed for reflection and rest.

Sloth is one of the seven deadly sins. For many of us raised with Christian ethics, rest, repose, and relaxation are not valued. Instead, they are judged as sloth, a mortal sin to be avoided at all costs. In *Purgatorio*, Dante ironically imagined penance for the slothful as nonstop running at high speed. In our reverence of looking busy, that's exactly what we do. We run nonstop at top speed to avoid sloth. We focus on doing as much as we can and giving as much of ourselves as possible.

When we focus on doing or giving rather than integrating in being and receiving, we fall out of balance. Being overly invested in the hustle and bustle of being occupied, we miss receiving important messages from God. God sends divine beauty in sunsets, strength in mountains, and peace in reflections in lakes. We only receive these when we take time to experience them. The ability to see the heaven that we live in relies on taking the time to step out of everyday activities to repose, rest, and reflect. Only then do we gain the opportunity to get in touch with our God-self that speaks in whispers.

With our crowded calendars, instant electronic communication, and compulsion to avoid sloth, we must create time to find God. We must create balance in our lives in order to be able to listen to ourselves and be receptive to God. Sometimes, we do need to sit like a bump on a log in order to feel the nudging of Divine Guidance.

GOD'S INVITATION: BALANCE

Look at the circus performer that juggles spinning plates on sticks. The juggler must keep the plates level and the sticks supporting them in a steady even position. Just like the juggler, we keep so many things spinning at once. With all the responsibilities of home, family, work, and social obligations, we multitask holding the whole gig together without letting it topple to crash down upon us.

If you feel the stress of juggling too much, you are not alone. *The Huffington Post* reported that 91 percent of people feel stressed. That high percentage screams out the need for balance.

Balance is a state of equilibrium. Balance is where the plates stay spinning in the air. It requires setting them in motion and then breathing while they do their job. To achieve balance in our lives, we must give time to doing and being. We must give time for giving and receiving. That helps us maintain healthy mental and spiritual harmony.

To put balance into your own life, start by building a Balance Survival Cupboard. This cupboard will hold workable strategies that can help maintain a healthy balance. Draw a cupboard on a piece of paper to serve as your Balancing Survival Cupboard. In your cupboard, write the boundaries that you want to set. Consider managing Time and Energy, two of the most important factors that cause our plates to come crashing down around us. The biggest challenge in dealing with time and energy management is working with no list, no boundaries, and trying to do it all. Nailing down each item on the list lets you corral everything that needs to fit into your cupboard.

- **Time:** Make a To-Do list each day. If the activity takes more than five minutes, it goes on the list. Prioritize the list by importance.

- **Energy:** Make a list of the people who demand energy from you. Consider family, friends, and social acquaintances. Again, prioritize these people in the order of importance to you.

Once you have made your lists and prioritized their elements, then you can address setting boundaries on your time and energy. Consider these solutions:

- **Develop routines to deal with mail, emails, phone calls, and texts at a specific set time**

every day. Set an allotted quiet time. Turn off ringers, beepers, phones, and all notifications to enable you to work undisturbed. If you don't hear notifications, you won't be tempted to leave your train of thought to answer. Handle each item only once. Take in the message and respond right then.

- **Keep one calendar.** Combine work and home calendars. You live one life that needs to be integrated.

- **Communicate.** Keep your family in your business loop, and keep your business a part of your family. Set realistic expectations.

- **Choose positive people.** We are made up of the five people that we spend 80 percent of our time with. Make these five be positive supporters who nourish you. Set boundaries for the social vampires who suck your energy. Avoid toxic people. Watch the negative energy that you allow. Set boundaries here also for time thieves. This is the most troublesome challenge, watch the people who interrupt you, dump stuff on you to do, or create worry.

- **Take care of your physical needs.** Nurture yourself. Take time for your physical needs not merely an occasionally massage. Create a daily routine of physical exercise and get plenty of sleep. Carve out time daily for quiet time: communion through meditation, yoga, music, journaling, or whatever activity enhances your spiritual development.

What falls by the wayside since you have neither time nor energy does not matter. No sense in clinging to detritus that clogs up your life. Instead, focus on protecting your time and energy in order to fulfill your destiny.

PRAYER

Dear Lord, I feel tugged in many directions with responsibilities. Please help me to maintain my priorities, fulfilling my mission here on earth. I know you will guide and direct me on my journey.

PART III

CELEBRATING G-VITES TO FIND HAPPINESS

Living In Gratitude

19
ATTUNING TO MINDFULNESS

The present moment is filled with joy and happiness. If you are attentive, you will see it. —Thich Nhat Hanh

"Never again," I vowed, hurling the cumbersome box onto the granite counter top. I mopped a bead of sweat from my brow. Moving into our new digs was not as I expected. For one, the hot Arizona fall made the work a chore. For another, the house wasn't living up to my expectations.

My husband, Joe, and I bought this new home for more living space. But as I unpacked the boxes marked Kitchen, frustration set in. The cupboards would not hold all my precious treasures. Antique platters, holiday dinnerware, and crystal goblets still tucked into their boxes with no place to put them. In the master bathroom, I'd reached the same point when I filled all the cupboards and drawers, but still had more boxes of beauty supplies to unpack.

We had remodeled our last house to add more storage space in the bathrooms and kitchen. After four remodels, including the baths and kitchen, plus rebuilding the pool, re-stuccoing the exterior, replacing the roof, and constructing a new laundry room, we still felt cramped. So we set out to find a bigger house.

The newer house, not too far away, came with a few drawbacks. We looked forward to enjoying its spaciousness, but it had a few quirks. While unpacking, I battled with the outdated small cabinetry, jamming all my beauty products (Joe says it takes a lot of time and money to look this natural) into the narrow inadequate drawers. I slammed drawers shut, longing for our previous remodeled storage that had so many personally designed comforts.

That first night in the new house, I searched for my normal view of the city lights. But dark landscaping greeted my southern exposure. With my nighttime view of dancing city lights gone, I checked the north side, staring into the gloomy darkness. My shoulders slumped in disappointment.

Looking into my rear view mirror, I longed for my previous home. I yearned for its big kitchen cupboards, large bathroom drawers, and the nighttime dazzle of city lights. In my new surroundings, an emptiness crept in to nip at the joy of moving into my new home. I flopped into bed, wondering if we had made a bad decision.

A good nights sleep brought a new perspective. That morning, I took a little time to explore. I threw open the north door of the house. What last night appeared as dark and gloomy lit up in the morning sun. Squaw Peak basked in an orange glow, looking as if I could run up it right from my own back yard.

"Where did this come from?" I spoke to the house since Joe had already gone into town. "How did I miss this beauty?"

The peak splayed out in morning radiance. In turn, its beauty greeted me with a fresh delight I had never experienced in my old house. I had been so caught up in my own feelings of what I didn't have that I completely overlooked what I did have. The house with its morning inspirational view was definitely the new wonderful.

The image of the sunlit peak clung with me for the remainder of my day. It chased away wallowing in the bog of negativity about what my new home lacked. I realized that looking backwards took my eye off the joy of my new home.

ATTUNING TO MINDFULNESS

How easily we lose sight of what we have before us! We slip from living an awe-filled life to surviving an awful existence. Life changing events, even ones that should bring joy, so often cause us to sink into regret. We perform litanies of lauding the good old days. We long for a future where things will be better. We are so distracted looking backwards or forward that we miss the moments of wonder where we can grasp joy.

Our lives are filled with wonderful every day. While happiness is not the end goal, it is the joy we find on our journey filled with everyday choices. Yes, happiness is a choice.

A 92-year-old man, who recently lost his wife, had to be admitted to a nursing home, since he no longer could live on his own. After patiently waiting to be shown to his new living quarters, the facility escort took the man's arm to lead him to his room. Walking through the corridor lined with doors decorated to make a home out of institutional living, the elderly gentleman commented on how much he liked his room. But they were only half way to their destination.

"But you haven't seen your room yet," said the young assistant. Surmising the gent's advanced age brought on confusion at the new place, she smiled at him.

"That doesn't have anything to do with it," the old man countered. "Happiness is something you decide on ahead of time."

The pair continued to shuffle down the hall. The young assistant looked askance at the old man, and he read her scrunched brow. "Whether I like my room or not doesn't depend on how the furniture is arranged...it's how I arrange my mind," the old man explained. "I already decided to love it."

His words packed a powerful punch—not just for the caregiver who heard them, but for us. Like the old man, we need to arrange our minds to look for the new wonderful, the happiness right there under our noses.

Happiness builds on being attuned to the gifts of the present moment rather than looking backward or forward. Nostalgia for the way things were robs us of time. Mulling on things we once owned, marathons we once ran, friends we once had, or carefree days of youth only keep our heads looking backwards. Similarly, dreaming of what we can do in the future if only a few things would fall into place lures us away from the present. Focusing backwards or forwards pulls us away from the new wonderful in the now.

We need to don those rose-tinted glasses and shift our minds into the happiness gear. Deciding to seek joy every day helps us enjoy what we do have and what does work in our lives. The present is indeed a present. And it's up to us to open the gift.

What's in the gift of being present? Mindfulness. We can be aware of the new wonderful offerings before us.

GOD'S INVITATION: MINDFULNESS

"Pay attention!" my teachers in grade school would admonish us. They meant for us to quit daydreaming or doodling in our notebooks and focus on the lesson at hand. Paying attention as we go through the day is important, but mindfulness goes a little further into the state of being conscious and aware.

Mindfulness operates as a discipline. Mindfulness engages us in purposefully living in the now. Casting away all judgments and expectations, we can live moment by moment. As we incorporate mindfulness, we gain a deeper understanding and appreciation of life: its stages, challenges, and joys.

The practice of mindfulness can be a learned skill. It starts by slowing down and bringing awareness into the present moment. It requires breathing deeply in one place rather than shuttling into nonstop go-go-go mode.

Simple mental and physical routines can add moments of mindfulness during the day. To begin incorporating mindfulness into daily routines, identify at least two regular physical things you do, such as driving the kids to school, brushing teeth, cooking dinner, or cleaning the house. Choosing two will give you specific times to add mindfulness into your day, rather than vaguely planning to remember to be mindful at undetermined times.

When you have decided on the two physical routines, it's time to add moments of mindfulness, the mental part, to the beginning of each one. Before each undertaking, focus your attention to the task at hand. Breathe deeply, and imagine what it looks like physically and mentally.

I opt for automatic absentminded actions to build mindfulness into my day: getting out of the car and answering the telephone. My head is always elsewhere during these two actions. Being mindful pulls me into the present for each one. Check out how they work for me:

GETTING OUT OF THE CAR

- My normal pattern: After parking the car, I grab my purse and other pertinent belongings from the passenger seat. Then, I dash from the car, rushing off to my destination.

- **My mindfulness pattern:** I check the passenger seat for my purse and such. But before I make a motion for the door handle, I stop. I sit still in my drivers seat to focus, taking three deep breaths. Slowing my activity, I recall just why I am going where I'm headed and what I want to accomplish. Then, I add a little affirmation, saying, "I know this will work out for the best." I slowly leave the car and mindfully walk to my appointment.

ANSWERING THE PHONE

- **My normal pattern:** When the phone rings, I usually drop everything that I am doing (even ceasing to type in the middle of a word). I grab the phone, while my head is still back on my typing.

- **My mindfulness pattern:** When the phone rings, I would slowly finish the typing of the word. Then, I take three deep breaths and smile. I pick up the phone anticipating a great conversation with the person calling.

With this attention to the present situation coupled with a focused positive energy, we can bring full awareness and positivity to each normally dull routine. With practice and repetition, we can train our minds to keep focused on the present and be less distracted by negative thoughts.

PRAYER

Dear Lord, I know you invite me to meet you in my everyday activities. Sometimes I get so wrapped up in them that I miss the opportunity to really appreciate the present moment. Help me to be mindful of the joy that surrounds me.

20
PRODUCING PATIENCE THROUGH GRATITUDE

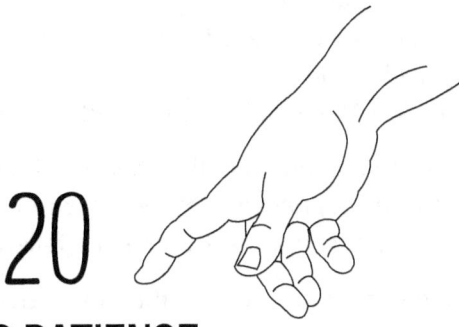

Patience is not simply the ability to wait; it's how we behave while we're waiting. —Joyce Meyer

Balancing the cheater glasses on the tip of my nose while straining to read the next item on my grocery list, I maneuvered the grocery cart down the aisle. Time spent in the supermarket ranks high as a necessary but unpleasant task. I aim to get in and get out quickly.

In a planned attack, I steer my cart up and down the aisles in a determined fashion. But the fresh fruits and vegetables baffle me. They seem to be tossed randomly on tables. I circle one table, and then another in search of my favorite apples.

The fresh produce section bewildered me. With the introduction of so many organic pieces of produce, apples now get stashed in three different sections: store brands, organic, and local farmers. Circling yet one more table, I spot my apples, select several, and tuck them in a plastic bag in my cart.

Filled with satisfaction at my list with every item crossed off, I make a beeline for the check out lanes. I avoid the self-check station, uncomfortable with the responsibility and lacking the extra time needed to learn the process.

Evaluating the length of the checkout lines and the speed of each checker, I rolled my cart into place behind several other shoppers. But the line failed to move.

Feeling frustration rise with the slow moving grocery queue, I tapped my foot on the floor. To occupy my mind, I analyzed the people with heaping shopping carts in the adjacent 10-items-or-less line. My growing impatience led to smart-ass thoughts: Were they literature majors who couldn't count, or math majors that couldn't read?

My queue crawled forward by inches while the heaping carts in the adjacent line filed past the cashier. "Crap," I tapped my foot more. I hate to waste time, an echo perhaps of the waste-not-want-not lessons from growing up. When my line finally inched forward past the magazine shelf, the tabloids displayed cover articles like "Dirty Divorces," "How to Lose 20 Pounds in 2 Days," or "The 50 Million Dollar Breakup." I rolled my eyes as the stories only emphasized how much time I was wasting.

Then, the productive button in my mind kicked on urging me to use the precious gift of time. Instead of occupying my mind with nonsense, I resorted to prayer. I started with gratitude:

"Thank you, Lord, for this food that I'm buying. Thanks also for the money to purchase what I need. Thank you for my body that works to digest this food into energy. Thank you for the checker standing trying to be pleasant to all. Thank you for the shelf stocking crews and the truck drivers delivering the food."

As I worked through everyone associated with my providing my food, time flew by. I reached the cashier and zipped out of the grocery with my bags. I walked to my car with my groceries, but pumped up with gratitude.

INSTANT IMPATIENCE

Many of us pray frequently for patience. If we could order patience from Amazon, we'd order a double dose and expect to receive it in record-breaking time. But because we can't buy patience, we beg God to help us. More than once I've caught myself praying, "God, please grant me patience. NOW."

Immediacy is part of our lives: Instagram pictures, quick microwave meals, instant messaging, prompt emails, Jiffy muffin mixes, rapid transit, overnight mail, urgent replies, critical responses, and ASAP notifications!

When we pray for patience, we also demand instant delivery of that patience. With our expectation of instant solutions, we get impatient when a solution takes time.

As our impatience mounts, we whirl out of control. Impatience breeds more impatience. With impatience with ourselves, it spills onto others and then God. Let's see how the pattern works:

IMPATIENCE WITH OURSELVES

We develop impatience with ourselves in many ways:

- **We fail to meet standards.** When we set high standards of perfection for ourselves, impatience grows with failing to meet the standards of being good enough, smart enough, or successful enough.

- **We exaggerate the urgency of immediate success.** We view time as slipping through our fingers rather than assessing what we can realistically achieve in the time we have.

- **We fail to acquire what we deem we need.** We get caught up in acquisition. We strive to acquire enough money and enough material goods.

- **We emphasize what we lack rather than what we have.** We focus on the time we lack instead of looking at how we can best use the time we have. We complain about the happiness we lack instead of seeking the small pieces of joy in our lives.

IMPATIENCE WITH OTHERS

Impatience with ourselves often spills over into impatience with others. People grate on us like fingernails on the chalkboard, especially when we perceive them to fail to meet our needs.

- **People fail to meet our time expectations.** We are in a hurry because our time is important, and others seem to be unable to recognize that. We get frustrated with sales clerks that seem to take an extraordinary amount of time doing their jobs and cars moving too slowly on the freeway.

- **People fail to see things the way we do.** We think people should immediately agree with the way we see things. We think our points are obvious, and we fail to understand their lack of enlightenment.

- **People fail to convert from their old ways of doing things into ways we think are better.** "That's the way we have always done it," they say. We get impatient with them for failing to make necessary and prudent changes.

- **People fail to keep up with us physically.** We lose patience walking behind slower amblers in crowds, waiting in lines for older or physically challenged people, and repeating comments for the hearing impaired.

IMPATIENCE WITH GOD

Like a spreading plague, our impatience carries over to God. We want our prayers answered on our schedules and in the manner we see fit.

- **We feel the crunch of time.** We have deadlines to meet, and God seems to be on a different schedule than us. We forget that God is on DST, Divine Standard Time.

- **We think we know what is best for us.** When God has a new lesson for us to learn or has something better for us in mind, we lose patience when the divine answer is other than we expect. We forget that God has the bigger plan and sees the whole picture.

Our impatience mounts until it consumes us. Instead of letting it run our lives, destroy our relationships with others, and keep us from bonding with God, we need to turn our impatience into patience.

GOD'S INVITATION: PATIENCE

How do we convert impatience to patience? Everywhere we turn requires patience. To gain patience, we must practice that state of being that sustains calmness, stability, and even-temperedness in difficult circumstances. Practicing patience will in turn suppress our restlessness when we are confronted with irritations and delays.

One of the underlying working principles in patience begins with the practice of gratitude. To practice gratitude, approach each situation with an open mind and open heart to count your blessings in the present. Two techniques can aid in cultivating gratitude. Using the Stream of Gratitude Prayer and creating a Facebook gratitude page can swap the focus on impatience to patience.

STREAM OF GRATITUDE PRAYER

A quick, easy prayer can keep you in the present moment offering thanks with an abundant heart. No memorization is needed. Rather than a recited prayer, use a self-created stream of consciousness list of thankfulness. Invent your own list. Here's how to do it:

- Start by letting your mind wander through what sits in front of you: food, people, homes, children, comforts, friends, families, or things.
- Bless whatever or whomever pops into your head.
- Give thanks for every item you think of.

The Stream of Gratitude Prayer can provide a vehicle to move you from an agitated state of impatience into a state of thankfulness. Shifting your thoughts to blessings in turn brings on an attitude of acceptance and peacefulness. Shift into a patient gear by practicing the steam of consciousness prayer.

GRATITUDE FACEBOOK PAGE

To encourage living with a grateful heart, design a Facebook page to share gratitude. The purpose of this page is to create a close circle of like-minded people who want to share and keep in touch through Facebook.

On a Facebook page I belong to, each person posts an item to be grateful for each day. Sometimes, it may be just the ability to get out of bed. Other times, we post bigger blessings. Our members comment in support of contributions. Sharing the gratefulness between us each day helps to focus our minds on gratitude. The process puts life into perspective and thus we find patience with ourselves, others, and God.

It's easy to create this gratitude-based community. Here's seven steps to creating your own gratitude community on Facebook:

1. Go to the Groups section on the left side of your home Facebook page.
2. Click on "add group," and then "create group."
3. Name your group, titling it with its mission: Thoughts of Gratitude, Daily Gratitude, or Giving Daily Thanks.
4. Invite members (You will need at least one member before you create your group).
5. Choose your privacy settings, choosing between

"anyone" being allowed to join, "closed" group, or "secret" group.

6. Click "create."
7. From there you can choose a group icon, complete the About section, and edit group settings when needed.

For communicating with your gratitude community, post something daily: an engaging image, quote, or question for member responses. Participate by responding to the posts of the other members.

Working the practice of gratitude into your day will help emphasis swap from impatience to patience. All good things come to those who wait...patiently.

PRAYER

Dear Lord, Grant me patience with myself, others, and you. Help me to remain in the state of gratitude by being accepting of each person and situation for what it is. Help me dismiss my expectations. Yes Lord, grant me patience NOW.

21
ANTICIPATING MIRACLES

Never forget that anticipation is an important part of life. Work's important, family's important, but without excitement, you have nothing. You're cheating yourself if you refuse to enjoy what's coming. —Nicholas Sparks

Tucking the bed sheet under my chin, I rolled over to maneuver into a comfortable position. The night left me tossing and turning. My restless thoughts grew from miniscule molehills into massive mountains. I caught the time on the digital alarm clock: 1:10, 1:46, 2:00 a.m. After the 2:30 reading, I must have finally conked out.

Chirping broke into my sleep. Tweets and trills elevated my consciousness out of its sleepy state. The clock read 4:15 a.m. I groaned at the birds. They warbled on in response.

"Don't they know it's still dark out and the sunrise is still a couple of hours away?" I complained to Joe, whose slow breathing indicated that he still slept deeply.

I flopped over in irritation. "If you want to greet the day, be quiet and begin the heralding later," I addressed the birds. "Right now, I need some sleep."

Covering my ears with the pillow, I mused on the singing birds, hoping they would put me back to sleep. But my thoughts could not turn off. I accused the birds of being unable to tell time, since darkness still seemed to prevail outside. Then, I wondered if perhaps they really could tell time.

That was it! My feathered friends were singing their hearts out in anticipation. They were celebrating the arrival of a new day. The birds honored the miracle that was about to occur. They were singing in anticipation rather than after the fact. Their melodies anticipated the miracle of another day.

With my lack of sleep, I had been engrossed in irritation at the birds. In doing so, I almost missed the lesson that they were teaching—to be a Miracle Seeker.

ANTICIPATING MIRACLES

Even before sunrise, the birds loudly proclaimed their anticipation of another miraculous day. We can take a lesson from the birds about when they start their songs and why they sing. They start singing in anticipation of the day and expect that the miracle of the day will occur.

We've all seen the bumper sticker: "Expect a miracle." We need to anticipate the miracles that surround our daily lives. We need to build the joyful exuberance of hope and sing about the expectation of a miracle in the gift of another day. Cultivating the Miracle Seeker in ourselves will help us begin each day in a positive frame of mind.

Miracle Seekers anticipate each day. Before our feet even hit the ground, as Miracle Seekers, we ready our minds for another inspiring day. Wonder fills our intellects with the potential of grand, glorious adventures God has planned. We get excited for the coming of the unknown. We mentally get in the ready position, like a tennis player ready to receive whatever volley comes his way.

Anticipation or the yearning for something good to come acts as a powerful tool for happiness. From the *Journal of Applied Research in Quality of Life*, a study shows how anticipation affects us. For instance, the largest boost in happiness comes from **planning** the vacation, more than the actual trip itself. The study even determined that the benefits of napping in bringing down a person's blood pressure are brought about **beforehand** merely by the anticipation of the nap rather than the actual siesta.

Anticipation, also called preconceived intuition, works also with food. When we smell the aroma of food, the mere anticipation of tasting the first morsel triggers salivation. Anticipation can be very healthy, the study found. It spurs us into the future with positive thoughts and a delightful sense of expectation.

Miracle Seekers naturally add anticipation to their days. Their minds and their hearts have to be in the ready position for whatever may happen. Miracle Seekers adopt an attitude of intent: they **want** to see, **expect** to see, and **intend** to see everything working for the highest good during the day.

As days go by, Miracle Seekers strive to remain grateful coupled with anticipation. No matter what happens, they try to find the silver lining, knowing that everything works out for the best. Eventually. Some miracles may take time.

Miracle Seekers take a grateful heart to bed in readiness for the next day. They thank God for the miracles of past 24 hours before dropping off to sleep. They anticipate more miracles to come the following day.

Over time, Miracle Seekers master the art of anticipating upcoming joys. Happy anticipation becomes a part of their personalities.

GOD'S INVITATION: ANTICIPATION

By emulating Miracle Seekers, we can accept the G-vite of anticipation. It builds on positive thinking, serving us throughout the day. It is the expectation of the likelihood of positive outcomes, conditions, and events. Envisioning positive outcomes is part of the process. We approach each situation with a faith that knowing the best is yet to come. Excitement builds. We can program ourselves for anticipation.

Music often creates anticipation. At the movies, certain background music lets the audience knows that something is about to happen. By its melody and tone, the music predicts what is about to take place. Spooky music denotes that some scary will occur, while romantic tunes culminate in a love liaison. Seasonally, music also creates anticipation; Christmas carols set the hopeful tone for the holidays. Music programs us to expect certain things to take place.

The same is true for anticipation. We can program ourselves to expect optimistic results. We can nurture anticipation through establishing routines. Following routines of successful people helps.

Many of the world's most successful people have a

daily morning routine to set themselves up for a productive day. Much like the birds, they set themselves up for a new day. In turn, they get what they expect.

For example, at day's start, motivational speaker Tony Robbins spends 15 minutes being grateful for what he has. This gratitude helps him identify what he wants out of life. When he understands and sees what exactly he wants from life, he builds a vision. He commits to his day with determination and the certainty being led by his goal.

"Take thoughts and turn them into actions, turn them into results, turn your dreams into reality," he explains. Robbins' morning routine builds anticipation that in turn creates miracles for his day.

Taking a page from Robbins' playbook, we can copy his morning routine. We can mimic his pattern for a 15-minute morning meditation. We can express gratefulness for what we have: family, friends, home, health, and jobs. Then, we can focus on what we want for the day. Then, we should develop a vision of the day and commit to it. By practicing this pattern, it will become ingrained in us. This habitual launching of the day can fill us with joy.

Sometimes, however, our days can get bogged down with errands, meetings, appointments, and lengthy to-do lists. So how do we build a routine of anticipation for these trying days?

Time management courses advocate making a list of tasks that need to be accomplished. This is a good place for us to start. We can create the same list, but then recast the activities for the day with a positive spin.

Start by writing the to-do list for the day. Then, take each item individually to restate it in positive terms. Those terms can reinforce anticipation and confidence in the outcome. Here's a classic task on our to-do lists:

—*Go to the grocery store.*

Listing the words "grocery store" implies a humdrum task of wheeling a cart up and down aisles while selecting vegetables, fruit, meat, bread, milk, and other necessities. The to-do list has already taken on a leaden feel, full of drudgery and boredom.

But now, let's give the task a positive spin with gratitude. With the grocery store task, we can envision those who cannot afford to buy food. That turns our word on the list into the following:

—*I GET to go to the grocery store.*

The words now express gratitude. That gratitude spills into turning the task from drudgery into an act of thankfulness. Other items on the to-do list can also change into gratitude. Instead of writing down the words "faculty meeting," spell it out with a positive spin.

Positive Spin: I have the opportunity to participate in a productive meeting that could help hundreds of kids.

Now, you try it. Recast items on your to-do list using the sentence starts below:

To-do List Item:

Positive Spin: This is the perfect time to…

To-do List Item:

Positive Spin: This task will bring…

By this simple task of rephrasing our to-do list, we can build on the anticipation of the oncoming day. Taking the time to recast your to-do list into forms of gratitude, you can garner more happiness from your routine projects. The gratitude infuses positive benefits.

Positive spins can help build enthusiasm for whatever comes our way. They revamp our wiring to be Miracle Seekers. We will be prepared to see the miracles that occur every day. Miracles happen all around us, and when anticipating them, we will be open to enjoying them.

PRAYER

Dear Lord, I know you have a grand and glorious adventure planned for me today. Help me to bring an excited heart filled with anticipation to my day today.

Creating Abundance

22
FORGING AHEAD WITH FAITH

Faith expects from God what is beyond all expectation.
—Andrew Murray

"Turn on the Duke," commanded 92-year-old Winnie from her makeshift bed in the living room.

I flipped on her favorite John Wayne movie and returned to the kitchen to finish tidying up from lunch. Wayne's Rooster Cogburn character would take us to 4:00, just in time to catch Rachael Ray's culinary delights on the Food Channel. The familiar drill repeated every Friday afternoon—lunch, movie, and foodie television—for the previous five months.

Winnie was a hospice patient suffering with terminal breast cancer. Making the end of life as pleasant as possible was my goal. Helping her in and out of her hospital bed, assisting her with bathroom needs, and strapping on her chest brace to keep her comfortable. I cinched the brace tightly to her thin deteriorating torso while the Duke raged on and Rachael Ray's show whetted our palates for dinner.

Winnie and I shared food, television, and a little about ourselves as the hours sped by. I learned about her family, her kids, the loss of her husband, and the death of her twins at birth. Life had not been easy for Winnie. No wonder she identified with her hero John Wayne and the Wild West.

As the closing credit rolled by on the screen, I turned off the television and propped myself in the chair beside Winnie's bed. She closed her eyes to sleep as I listened to her laborious breathing, far from rhythmic. A few minutes later, she awoke. She stared out into space, unaware of me and lost in her own world of thoughts. When she finally did look my way, I detected fear in her cloudy eyes.

"Are you okay?" I probed. "You look apprehensive."

"Yes, I'm just a little melancholy. I'm just not sure of what is coming next."

"Are you afraid of dying?" I held my breath broaching the subject.

"Yes." Usually she seemed such a strong character, so speaking of her vulnerability surprised me.

"Aren't you excited to get to heaven and see your husband, your parents, your siblings, and especially your twins?"

"I'm not sure that I'll see them. I believe that I will see

God, but not sure of anything else."

My heart sank at her words of spiritual doubt. Her faced furrowed in pain. Each wrinkle showed the uncertainly, the fear, and the apprehension of what lay ahead.

"It's going to be a grand reunion," I tried to reassure her. "All your loved ones, friends, and family, and even your animals will welcome you home to Heaven." The muscles in her face seemed to relax as we painted the glorious homecoming together.

"And when you get there, save a place for me, right next to you and the Duke," I added.

"I'll do just that." She closed her eyes and drifted into a peaceful sleep.

HAVING FAITH

I'm sure that Winnie is not alone in her feelings of unsteadiness, making her way on the last part of the journey. Since no one can tell us for certain the form that life will take, that's where faith comes in.

Saints, mystics, and spiritual leaders write about the dark night of the soul: where even the best and holiest of them experience painful doubts, even the very existence of God. Because of their faith, they interpret this darkness as an invitation to totally surrender their minds to reaffirm their faith, moving deeper into the mystery of the unknown.

We need an abundance of faith to embrace the seen and unseen, the known and unknown, in this life and the next. Developing this belief calls forth our faith in God's abundance—His caring and His love for us.

In *Encounters with Heaven*, Karin J. Gunderson shows evidence of God's abundant caring and love for us. She volunteers as a hospice harpist to visit the rooms of the dying. Karin has played for hundreds of people on their deathbeds, which has helped her gain certitudes about God.

Two of her observations demonstrate God's continuing love and caring.

1. **No one dies alone.** This is reassuring for someone like Winnie. While surrounded by friends and family her entire life, she suddenly found herself facing death alone. Even if earthly companions leave us alone, God provides us comfort with angels, friends, and loved ones from the other side as we transition through death.

    Author Marilyn Mendoza, Ph.D., reaffirms what I experienced in my own hospice work, that we do not die alone. In her book, *Jesus Is Coming to Get Me in a White Pickup Truck*, she chronicles accounts of nurses who were present at bedside deaths. Numerous nurses relate that their patients had the ability to see an essence from the Spirit world that calms fears, making the transition easier. This interaction with the "other side" not only reduces anxiety of the dying, but also provides peace and closure to their families.

2. **We are loved by God.** God cares about our personal needs, and nothing we do or don't do changes that. I find this certitude very comforting. It removes fear that an old white-haired deity is sitting behind the ledger of my life counting

> my sins and failings, like Santa Claus, tallying up my naughty or nice behaviors.
>
> We need to replace that fearful image with the persona of the father in the account of the Prodigal Son in the Bible. This father figure symbolizes grace and mercy. After his wayward son took his inheritance, ran off, and spent all of his money having a good time, he returned home. Deserving of his father's wrath, the son was surprised that his father met him instead with welcoming arms. This father portrayed the joy, forgiveness, and unconditional love that we will meet at the end of our journey. We are God's beloved children returning home.

By holding on to these two precepts, we can remove the fear surrounding death. Then, we can change our attitude toward the process.

In our hospice training, we were taught that there are two miracles in life: birth and death. We really celebrate the former, but need to celebrate the latter, too. If we keep faith and positive beliefs in mind as we live now, maybe at our end, we will be able to celebrate the last part of the journey with a strong belief, casting all doubts aside.

GOD'S INVITATION: FAITH

Faith builds on a strong confidence in someone or something. It's a trust in things unseen and out of the ordinary. The unknown can eat away at faith, pulling us away from what we believe to be true. But how do we develop, build, and strengthen faith?

Don't wait until your death for an infusion of faith. Faith-building is a lifetime exercise. By answering

God's invitations throughout each day, we will be ready for the big invitation at the end.

Death is a natural part of life. The unknowns as Winnie stated are what put the sword of fear in our minds, so we need to remove as much of the unknown as possible, building our faith in God's process.

Through three activities, we can engage in the here and now to help strengthen our faith. We can read, enroll, and nourish.

Read to gather as much information as you can. Start by tackling best sellers about death and grief:

- *Being Moral* by Atul Gawande
- *Tuesdays with Morrie* by Mitch Album
- *You Can Heal Yourself* by Louise Hay
- *Wherever You Go, There You Are* by Jon Kabat-Zinn
- *Healing After Loss: Daily Meditations* by Martha Whitmore Hickman
- *When Bad Things Happen to Good People* by Harold S. Kushner
- *Final Gifts: Understanding the Special Awareness, Needs, and Communication of the Dying* by Maggie Callanan and Patricia Kelley
- *Tear Soup: A Recipe for Healing After Loss* by Pat Schwiebert
- *The Last Dance: Encountering Death and Dying* by Lynne Ann DeSpelder
- *I Wasn't Ready to Say Goodbye* by Pamela D. Blair

Read these books, share them with friends, and give them as gifts. They provide great discussion fodder for book clubs. We need to talk about the elephant in the room—death—in order to strip away the unknown and build our faith in the entire life process.

Enroll in a hospice course. The introductory hospice course should be required for every person. Hospice teaches us the process of dying that we will we eventually face and assists us with knowledge and skills for dealing with our loved ones who are making the transition.

Hospice curriculum includes assistance in three areas: the patient, the family, and bereavement. The classes explain the dying process and stages involved. They emphasize helping the patient live while dying and dispelling the myths about death.

Their guide to grief explains the steps involved in the grieving process along with managing fears and anxiety. The guide addresses the family, regarding how to talk with children about death, what happens when a parent dies, and how to help the surviving children. We learn how to heal after loss.

The training program also includes patient rights, hospice and nursing homes, safety and infection control, family, Alzheimer's Disease, and spirituality and spiritual care. Learning about end of life issues can help us understand the natural occurrence of death. We can turn the process of dying into a celebration, preparing the patient, friends, and family for the beauty to come.

Nourish your relationship with your Creator each day. Using G-vites, talk, communicate, and build a connection with the Divine. Build the bond between you and your Creator, so when you do transition to the other side, it will be like a real homecoming. Meeting God should be like reuniting with a wonderful friend that you've missed for years. We can look forward to the second miracle in life, death, knowing that it is a next step in a personal relationship with God.

PRAYER

Dear Lord, help me to nourish my relationship with you, knowing that my death will be a fulfillment and glorious reunion.

23

LIVING IN ABUNDANCE

God will overflow your cup, so grab the biggest one you can find. —Rob Liano

To make room for later arrivals, I gathered my purse next to me and slid across to the middle of the pew. I had arrived at our San Diego church earlier than usual to get a good seat up front for the annual confirmation message from our bishop. He visited once a year to administer the sacrament of confirmation, bringing crowds of people streaming into the church.

As the bishop entered the rear of the sanctuary to commence celebration of the Mass, the congregation stood. The pungent aroma of incense filled my lungs. While the organ piped music fit for a king, the bishop made his way down the center aisle. He donned rich vestments embroidered for his sole use. I wondered if the accusations of his excessiveness had some substance.

Nearly two decades earlier, the public had accused him of extravagance in building The Immaculata. Editorials and feature articles plagued the *San Diego Union* during its construction. As head of the San

Diego Diocese, he had to answer for the amount of money spent on the church.

Although I'd never stepped foot in the Immaculata, located on the University of San Diego campus, I'd heard plenty about it. Dedicated in 1959, the Immaculata imitated the giant wealthy churches in Europe with a solid bronze front door, a 300-pound cross at the apex of the 167-foot-high bell tower, an 8,500-pound statue of Our Lady of the Immaculate Conception on top of the church's dome, and 50- to 105-foot-high ceilings. The interior contained 20 side-chapels with the Stations of the Cross imported from Europe, marble pillars and altars, and a hand-carved crucifix from Germany. With seating for 900 in the elegant surroundings, the church shot to the top location for weddings in San Diego.

During construction, the public had put the bishop and the Catholic Church on notice. Some called for a strict accounting of expenditures. Others decried the décor as too lavish and failing to serve the poor as Jesus did. The city at large wanted an explanation. I wondered if he had ever answered for the extravagance; if so, I had never heard about it. My speculation went no further.

At the front of the church, the bishop removed his miter, the hat designating the office of bishop. He led us in the familiar prayers and responses. About half way through the service, he began the homily with the usual blessings. Then, he launched into his confirmation message.

The bishop gestured slowly to take in the scope of our church. "Whenever you look at this church and others like it that brim over with extravagance, remember

God's love for you is just like that: over the top, way out of line, and above and beyond our expectations," he addressed us. The leader of the Catholic Church in San Diego had not dodged the barbs hurled at him. In fact, he admitted to extravagance and turned it into an accounting of God's love for us. While he addressed us in our church, he clearly referred to the Immaculata as a metaphor for how God's love for us is over-the-top abundant.

From under the beautiful vestments, he extended his outstretched arms. "God loves you this much," he spread his arms as broad as possible. "Let this church be a constant reminder of God's excessive love for each of us."

He directed his message at those being confirmed into the Catholic Church, but it reverberated through everyone. The bishop standing with his arms wide-open mirrored the arms of Christ on the crucifix above him. Even though nearly 40 years have passed since I heard the bishop speak, the image of the bishop and Christ on the cross, with both of their arms outstretched, stuck with me as visual representations of God's abundant love.

LIVING IN ABUNDANCE

When we think of abundance, wealth immediately comes to mind. The Immaculata Church, in all its glory, stands as a reminder that we live in abundance. But we can be abundant in other ways. Consider health, joy, happiness, family, friendships, sense of purpose, and liveliness. Abundance permeates our lives even without wealth.

Consider the story a local television reported last year. An airport janitor found an iPad with $13,000 cash stuffed inside the case. Instead of pilfering the cash, he turned in the iPad with the cash intact to his supervisor.

When the man who lost his iPad and money came to the Lost and Found to claim his missing items, he immediately checked to see if the cash was there. He found the currency precisely as he had left it, stuffed inside the case. Every dollar of it was there. The gentleman rewarded the airport employee with $60.

While most of us might consider blowing the $60 on dinner and drinks, the airport janitor had another plan. He gave his reward away, bestowing it on a fellow airport worker in a financial bind who needed it more.

The airport janitor operated out of the belief of abundance. I would bet that he could also have used the $60 for necessities of his own. But he approached life believing that there is enough: enough money, enough material goods, and enough of what he needed. His actions define the true meaning of abundance.

He lived with a grateful, loving heart in spite of a challenging job. Working at the airport as a janitor, he's no doubt seen humanity at its worst—angry, demanding, hurried, selfish, unobservant, and caught up in attaining material goods. But the janitor did not get caught up in the need for more, newer, or bigger things. He celebrated true abundance.

He celebrated abundance by choosing an outward vision that saw the needs of others. We can all take a lesson from the airport janitor. We celebrate abundance by paying attention to the needs of others that surround us rather than the acquisition of material wealth. The janitor did not need to horde material goods when he approached life with an abundant attitude, knowing that somehow, somewhere God will take care of him. We, too, can approach our daily lives with knowing that God will take care of us, thus creating a life of abundance.

"Today I behold all the abundance that surrounds me," says Deepak Chopra. His affirmation reinforces the presence of abundance in our lives.

GOD'S INVITATION: ABUNDANCE

Considering abundance, we usually think of plentiful visions: cornucopias of produce at Thanksgiving, mounds of packages under Christmas trees, tables laden with food, closets stuffed with clothes, and recreational equipment filling our garages. Over sufficient quantities come to mind; they are quite the opposite of scarcity.

When I look at my life, I know I live in abundance. But living in abundance is more than knowing I'm blessed. It requires a daily attention to abundance rather than a vague thought gathering cobwebs in the back closets of the mind.

To ensure I maintain living in this spirit of abundance, I begin each day by filling my Gratitude Jar. When I first read about this activity on Facebook, I shrugged the Gratitude Jar off. "How elementary," I scoffed. "Why do I need to use a Gratitude Jar when I know I live in abundance." But I tried it anyway. In the process, I discovered its role in keeping one's mind on daily abundance.

Here's how I use my Gratitude Jar. Each morning, I take three sticky notes and jot on each paper one thing that I am grateful for from the previous day. Then, I deposit the notes in a tall iris vase with a big black and white bow.

My sticky notes document the daily blessings. My notes contain positive memories, funny moments that made me laugh, beauty in nature, accomplishments, small successes, words from friends, or pleasant surprises. Adding these notes reinforces my true abundance daily.

That's the process. Now, granted I've only been at this for a few months, but I've found amazing results already.

First of all, I find myself looking for things to be grateful for during the day. Instead of focusing my attention on negatives, I find myself looking for positives. This puts me in a frame of mind to look for the good in every day.

Second, when I put my head on my pillow at night, I reflect on the day in order to decide what three blessings to write down the next morning. I fall asleep while my subconscious is focused on all the wonderful things that have filled my last 24 hours. Instead of worrying about what I did or did not accomplish that day, I find a sense of relaxation knowing that I'm truly blessed.

Lastly, my tall vase sitting on my desk is a constant visual reminder of the true abundance in which I live. Every once in a while, I dip into the contents of my Gratitude Jar to read all those little sticky notes. They, in turn, give me a reason to pray in thankfulness—to thank God for the abundance provided for me.

Dig through your closet to find an urn that you can use for your own Gratitude Jar. You can decorate it however you see fit, but put it in a place that you will see daily. That will encourage you to add three blessings daily. A Gratitude Jar can also become a family routine, with each member contributing his or her own messages of abundance. For children, the process instills gratefulness. You can also encourage visitors to contribute to your Gratitude Jar. When people come into my office at my house, I invite them to take a second to jot down one thing that they are grateful for today.

Abundance does surround us. Let's rejoice, be glad, and acknowledge our wonderful gifts.

PRAYER

Dear Lord, I know that I am loved and cared for by an all-knowing Creator, giving me exactly what I need for my journey. I live in the wealth of your love and surrounded by abundance.

24

MAINTAINING WONDER

I have long thought that anyone who does not regularly— or ever—gaze up and see the wonder and glory of a dark night sky filled with countless stars loses a sense of their fundamental connectedness to the universe.
—Brian Green

"Ready to go?" I asked Joe, as I finished double tying the shoestrings on my tennis shoes and grabbed my wide brimmed hat for our daily walk. When we lived in Montana, my husband and I started each summer day with an early morning three-mile trek up to the water tower on the top of Lion Mountain where we lived.

Swinging open the side door leading to the street, I took in the canopy of gray sky. "Guess we can skip the sunglasses today," I hollered back to Joe.

As I looked outside, Joe poked around the corner to join me. He eyed the clouds, which grew darker and more foreboding. Misty sprinkles came down, then several droplets. Joe stalled.

"Nope, think I'll pass today," he spun around to

retreat back into the house. "We have so many better days than this."

While Joe retreated to his office, I grabbed my umbrella and my phone, just in case the heavens broke loose with a deluge. I paused for a moment, wondering just what Joe meant by the word "better." We usually enjoyed the outdoors in the sunshine, but I remembered running around as a kid in the rain with the rich earthy smell it called forth from the ground and wondered if I could still smell that richness as adult.

"Keep your phone handy, hon," I lobbed my parting words to Joe. "Just in case I need a lift. I'll call for a pick up if the heavy stuff comes down."

Hoisting my umbrella, I headed off up the street. Raindrops plopped around me, splatting on the pavement and pattering on the fabric of my umbrella. I savored the clean air and inhaled that same damp smell of the earth, just like when I played in the rain as a kid. I marched in time to the raindrops hitting my umbrella. The clouds morphed into shapes of animals, and their changing shapes merged into new beasts. I relished the alone time with just my thoughts, the rain, and the animals in the sky.

About half way up the hill to the water tower, only 15 minutes from my house, the clouds began to shift faster. Within a few more steps, they whooshed eastward toward Glacier Park, like they were late for some weather appointment. Luminous rays of sunshine shot through thin holes in their vapors, causing me to shield my eyes. Minutes later, the haze drifted away, firing up the radiance of the sun.

I took a deep breath of rain-scented air and shook the drops off my umbrella. The beauty of the forested mountain lit up. Wet foliage glistened, and the world seemed renewed.

"I should have brought my sunglasses after all," I spoke to myself while soaking up the splendor. "Poor Joe, waiting for a better day. How does it get any better than this? No wonder in Montana, people always say, 'Wait five minutes, and the weather will change.'"

MAINTAINING WONDER

The very first CD I bought for Joe contained the song, "I Hope you Dance," by Lee Ann Womack. She belted out the lyrics, "I hope you never lose your sense of wonder, you get your fill to eat, but always keep that hunger, may you never take one breath for granted…"

Womack nailed how we take so much for granted. Like her song, my walk in the rain reiterated the importance of seeking out moments of wonder even in sour conditions.

Because we take so many aspects of life for granted, we lose a sense of wonder in everyday joys. We forget about maintaining the sense of wonder for daily occurrences in our lives: spending time with family and friends, eating food that nourishes us, and soaking up the beauty that surrounds us in nature.

Two roadblocks thwart us in maintaining our sense of wonder. Womack addresses the first one with **taking things for granted**. It is so easy for us to slip into taking people, circumstances, or even the next breath for granted. When we take daily occurrences for granted, we cannot maintain a sense of wonder.

We know intellectually that we need to pay attention to the little things in our lives, but emotionally we take our health, jobs, and lives for granted. We roll along assuming things will never change. When something occurs out of the ordinary, like loss of a job, illness or death, we feel like the rug has been pulled out from under us. We lose our sense of balance. We fight to maintain a sense of normalcy. In reality, those tragedies are part of life. They always reinforce how we cannot take our health, jobs, or lives for granted.

The second roadblock is our **expectations**. We expect that things will stay the same. So, we all wait for that better day to do things we want. We wait until we are married, or have kids, or when the kids leave for college. We wait until we have finished school, lose ten pounds, pay off the house, or retire. We bide time waiting for the weekend. We tend to think that things will be better in the future when our situations improve, settling for the way things are. This optimism serves us well, but can act as a roadblock to happiness. By focusing on the future, we can miss the beauty that is right before our eyes.

Our expectations impede our journey to happiness by bringing our calculated perspective to the situation. We have little room for anticipation of a different outcome. In doing so, we get what we expect—mundane life—with little chance for surprise wonders.

Taking things for granted and expecting the mundane suck the sense of wonder right out of us. With both, we get bogged down in moderation, when we should relish living in awesome.

Maintaining a sense of wonder in the present moment helps us discover the beauty of something strange and surprising. It can serve as a springboard for saving the sweetness of life, the joie de vivre. Circumstances are the same, all part of the same picture. But when we change the lens, we can discover the gift of the present moment.

Like the fast-changing weather in Montana's mountains, life can gain wonder in one second, one phone call, or one walk up the hill.

GOD'S INVITATION: WONDER

Remember the Christmas joke about the child opening his present? He wildly tears open the wrapping paper only to find a box of horse manure. With enthusiasm, he plunges into the box, exclaiming, "If there is all this manure, there must surely be a pony in here somewhere!" The child expects the best.

Somehow life's experiences weigh heavily on adults… to the point of wiping out wonder. Over the years, we become more rational, saner, and more realistic. We lose the exuberance of childhood. We feel bound by the conventional, fitting the norm, and marching to the accepted drummer.

As adults, we need to shift our paradigms. We can't go back in time to recapture the sense of wonder. So we need to take the sense of wonderment from childhood and switch on its breaker in our everyday lives. Since we have been so conditioned to seek approval from others, we may need to make a concentrated effort to step out of our comfort zone to establish new parameters and rekindle wonderment.

It's all about the lenses with which we choose to view our lives. We can opt for a variety of emotional colors:

clear realism, cynicism, resentment, anxiousness, frustration, fearfulness, hesitation, or resistance, for example. When we choose the lenses, such as a pair of rosy-colored glasses, we can choose those that yield more joyful ways of looking at the world—with kindness, hopefulness, and gratitude.

When you control the lenses, you can change your perceptions. Don a pair of rose-tinted glasses to practice seeing your world in a more upbeat manner. Find the best in the people who come in and out of your day. Look for the nugget of wonder in the situations that you encounter daily.

Beginning to change lenses may take practice. Set aside a few minutes at night to review your day, itemizing people and events with their most positive elements. In a way, you are creating a Pollyanna Newspaper for your day. Pollyanna, from the 1913 book by Eleanor H. Porter, made the technique famous with her Glad Game in which she aims to glean at least a tidbit of gladness in every thing that happens.

Write down your column for the day. Take judgment and expectation out of the recounting. Observe events as if you were a third party digging for a gold nugget. Avoid sarcasm, but employ a good PR spin if needed to add the spice of wonder. Even if your event is unpleasant, just plain dark, or even debilitating, look for that small ray of light. Spin your story so it paints a joyful ending, even if that ending is only a tiny ray of hope.

Since we need to "Bloom where we are planted," we must find joy in our present circumstances. Not later, but NOW. In tough situations, an immediate goodness may not be there. In that case, quote King Solomon, who reputedly had an inscription on his ring that read, "This too shall pass."

Just like the child looking for the pony in the box of manure, we need to seek out wonder. Find those moments of delight, and focus on those. These moments of wonder are G-vites from God.

PRAYER

Dear Lord, You are full of surprises. Keep my sense of wonder sharp, ever seeking your beauty and joy, finding delight in every circumstance.

Cultivating Happiness

25
GAINING FREEDOM THROUGH RELEASE

Everybody thinks of changing humanity, but nobody thinks of changing himself. —Leo Tolstoy

When Joe and I married in 1992, we were not young teens running off into the sunset mimicking some romantic movie. We brought age, experience, and hopefully a little wisdom to our new relationship.

Neither of us had aced the classes presented in the school of life. Joe had been married twice before, and I, too, had two marriages—one as a nun to God and after the convent, one to a man. The baggage we dragged with us came from hard knocks.

Both in our forties, we brought strengths and weaknesses to our new union with the intention of building a long happy life together with the time we had left.

We approached married life knowing our responsibilities, ready to accept the duties as husband and wife.

For years, our home ran smoothly on the division of labor theory. Working from traditional role models, Joe assumed the part as provider, producer, and protector. Watching over the family finances and being Mr. Fix-It fell on his side of the ledger. On my side of the to-do list was most everything else—social engagements, cooking meals, doing laundry, and, of course, making the bed. I don't mind making our bed. When single, I made my own bed, so taking on that task created no added responsibility. Smoothing the sheets and blankets into place helped me kick-start my day. The process sets the tone for being organized, neat, and orderly for the rest of my daily tasks.

But one day, the scales tipped. As an elementary school principal, I had to hit the road earlier than usual to meet with some parents. I arose and hustled off the work, leaving Joe in bed.

When I arrived home later that evening, I saw the unmade rumpled bed. I assumed that the last one out would make the bed, if I were gone. Guess not.

For some reason, the unmade bed ate at me like a crawfish nibbling away at its prey. Resentment grew, and I huffed, "I always have to do everything." To alleviate my resentment, I promised myself to ask for assistance in the bed-making task next opportunity.

A week later, another early morning appointment loomed. While getting into bed, I broached Joe with the subject of making the bed in the morning.

"Hey, hon, since you are going to be the last one out

of bed, would you mind making the bed?" The words came out far more timid that I meant.

"Sure, no problem," he complied with my wishes, polite as usual.

"Well, that was easy," I thought to myself. "Why hadn't I asked sooner? Why did I let this make-the-bed molehill morph into a mountain of resentment for me?"

After returning home the following evening and entering the bedroom, I saw that the bed was indeed made, but the numerous pillows were arranged all wrong. The square ones belonged behind the round ones, and the colors needed to alternate. Grabbing the pillows, I set out to make it right, placing each pillow in its correct positions.

Just as I finished, Joe entered the bedroom. He scrutinized what I had done. He looked at me and lobbed, "Now you know why I don't make the bed."

SEEKING RELEASE

So often we want to control little things in life, like me with the pillow arrangement on our bed. But we need to let go of the control button. Controlling all the small details cuts into our personal peace, joy, and connection with others.

For controllers, there is one right way of doing things, like the order of the pillows on our bed. Too much control can be toxic. On the list of toxic people, the control freak sits near the top. Instead of creating peace, they surround themselves with tension that others can feel. Instead of joy, they spew negativity at incorrect details. Instead of connecting with others, controllers push other people away with their demand for perfection their way. Around controlling people, we walk on pins and needles afraid that we will do something incorrectly and fearful of repercussions.

When we operate from our preconceived ideas of how things must be, we make other people and ourselves miserable. Control drops tidbits of misery in little ways. We load the dishwasher a certain way, but when visitors load it for us, we get miffed that dishes weren't loaded in their proper places, and our company feels our lack of gratitude. Control creates misery in larger ways, too. We funnel our kids into programs and careers that we think are best for them. They suffer in trying to please us, and then we sink into disappointment when they want to do something else.

When I get controlling, Joe resorts to a golf analogy. "Loosen your grip," he suggests. I understand the destructive consequences implied. When I clench a tight grip on the golf club, my swing results in a jerking motion that redirects the club head toward a skewed angle rather than in a direct line to the green. A tight grip indicates that I'm trying to steer the ball, but my swing ends up producing just the opposite. My ball steers off course.

I get Joe's analogy. I need to loosen my grip on my golf club, and in life I need to let go of the details to allow things to happen on their own accord. Unfortunately, Joe's golf analogy comes back at me time and time again. Having been raised in the theory that there is one right way and one right answer, releasing control is difficult for me.

Control is rooted in fear, distrust, and unworthiness. Check out how these three elements work:

- **Fear:** We are fearful of unexpected outcomes. We fear people who do not agree with us. We are afraid that we will not be able to handle whatever comes our way. We feel our world will fall apart if we let go.

- **Distrust:** We lack trust that problems can have multiple solutions. We lack trust in the judgment and decision-making of others. We distrust those who are different.

- **Unworthiness:** We experience a lack of self-esteem, weighing the possibilities that we will fall apart if we don't control everything. We lack the confidence to rise above potential hardships that may result from a decision.

These three emotions give rise to the need to control. We can begin to release control by recognizing their roles in our lives.

GOD'S INVITATION: RELEASE

God invites us to let go. We can let go of expectations and traditional ways things should be done. We need to release, go with the flow, and relax in the Lord, knowing that all will be well.

Experiencing true freedom only comes when we forgo micro-managing the situations around us. Releasing control frees our minds to be open to incoming intuitive communications and messages from God. When we are not obsessing about details, we have a quiet receptive presence of mind.

We can take a lesson from my grandmother. Every summer, my sister and I visited my grandparents in South Dakota. My grandfather commanded respect, and his ample frame supported his demeanor. My grandmother, on the other hand, was mild mannered. She was that peacekeeper that Jesus talked about in the Beatitudes. Her life was dedicated to placating everyone to avoid conflict, so much so that she metaphorically carried a white flag of surrender stuffed in her bra to wave at the least provocation.

Not used to kids in her house, my grandmother shifted into a different mode when we visited. Her discomfort with us in the house playing, arguing, and potentially upsetting my grandfather turned her into Nervous Nellie. Whenever anyone even hinted at an argument or voiced an alternate opinion, my grandmother would interject, "What difference does it make?"

Grandma could diffuse any situation with that simple question. My sister and I would drop our differences. Her question pointed out that our squabble didn't make any difference in the big scheme of life. Adopting that question can help put control issues in their proper place.

If you have been a control freak by birth order, religion, or upbringing, you will need to incorporate a new way of approaching people and situations gradually. Compile a list of ways to let go of routines and expectations, step by step. Start with everyday routines to see which ones lend to change. After all, it's easier to start on small things before tackling bigger situations.

Start with **small steps**. Don't make the bed on Sundays. Take an alternate route to work. Part your hair on the other side of your head. Change up the arrangement of things on your desk. Most of these are control routines that when changed, will affect only you.

When the small steps feel okay, then move on to **larger steps**. Refrain from commenting to companions when you see someone different, such as strange dress, tattoos, or body piercings. Step outside yourself and your opinions by watching another television channel or reading an alternative magazine for news presenting a different vantage point. Expose yourself to alternate points of view.

When you feel comfortable with larger steps, then move on to **giant steps**. These are the hardest ones as they involve releasing control of what you want others to do. Let go of trying to control kids and family members. Instead of telling them what you think they should do, find small tidbits of their choices that you can support and voice that.

When panic sets in at the lack of control, play the Extreme Game. This game looks at the situation and poses the question, "What's the worst thing that could happen?" Breathe, relax, and answer the question. The worst thing that can happen is most likely not even an outcome that you can control.

Only when we release control, can we begin to go with the flow. Floating on the river is more peaceful than fighting the current. Only then can we enjoy the variety that the world has to offer. As a bonus trade off, others will enjoy us, too.

PRAYER

Dear Lord, help me to expand my horizons accepting situations and people who stretch my narrow thinking. Let me release all expectation of outcomes, happy with whatever you send me.

26
LAUGHING TOWARD OPTIMISM

It's not that optimism solves all of life's problems; it is just that it can sometimes make the difference between coping and collapsing. —Lucy Macdonald

"Oh excuse me," a woman mumbled apologies as she forced her way in front of me. The crowd pressed toward the Phoenix auditorium entrance, with people pushing forward, unconcerned about cutting off others in line.

Frightful memories returned of a Super Bowl street party. The thick throng of partiers carried me along with my feet failing to scrape the ground. Panic stole my breath, and I had to look up to the sky to swallow oxygen. I begged God for safe passage.

But this crowd, almost churchlike in comparison, inched toward the ballroom doors in a more subdued swarm. Conversations swirled in muted tones, with eye contact nil and interactions with strangers at a minimum. This disparate group of people seemed to have only a love for comedy in common. I, for one, came to cross one thing off my bucket list—to see Jay Leno in person.

Inside the arena, my excitement returned as I entered the room with a lone microphone on the stage. Filing to our seats like quiet parishioners at church, we sat with care, avoiding any contact with the person sitting next to us. I sat up tall in my chair to take up less room, a feat made almost impossible with the seats being so tightly packed. Most of the audience sat isolated as individuals, keeping to themselves and awaiting the performance.

But soon the vibe changed. Jay walked on stage to loud applause. He launched into his usual monologue, sparing no one as the butt of his jokes. Jay's performance inspired us to laugh at ourselves in the everyday workings of family life. He related how as children we embarrassed our parents; then years later, our parents embarrassed us.

He prompted us to see the humor in our daily frustrations. He regaled us with stories of people who failed to see what was right under their noses. We roared as Jay connected us with laughter at our shared humanity. We cackled at nose hairs, bodily functions, growing older, losing our appeal, and our ineptness in dealing with technology. On and on, we howled at silly little things in ourselves. Our laughter connected us with the humanness that we all share.

Two hours flew by. After the performance, I felt drained, like after a hefty workout. My stomach ached, but with a good ache from laughing so hard. I turned to the lady next to me that I had totally ignored before the show, and we chatted like old friends. We lauded Jay's performance and asked each other if the experience was a first for us. We shared where we lived. We tittered together in shared moments of joy. Jay's comedy broke down barriers that were present prior to the performance.

Spilling out of the ballroom, this audience that earlier functioned as detached individuals bubbled with energy. Small groups mingled to share chuckles. Smiles stretched across everyone's faces as we had all witnessed the power of laughter.

In laughing at the absurd, ridiculous, or illogical aspects of our lives, we dropped the masks we usually wear in public for strangers. Laughter helped us share moments of joy, a taste of the Spirit—even with total strangers.

LAUGHING TOWARD OPTIMISM

What accounted for this major mood swing as we filed out of the arena—one minute as strangers and the next minute a community? Laughter! Laughter is a powerful tool.

The magazine staple *Readers' Digest* had a section called "Laughter is the Best Medicine." It contained humorous quips that captured the absurdities of life: the ridiculous, the irrational, the illogical, and the just downright silly. That article was the first section that my family dog-eared when the periodical arrived at our house. Some read only that, similar to those who read only the comics in the Sunday newspaper. We all needed a good laugh to keep life in perspective.

Looking at the lighter side of life can turn our beliefs around to give us new perceptions and novel ideas. We can shift our thinking to promoting hope and new resolve when we drop the heavy burden of taking ourselves so seriously. Laughter works as the antidote for fear, separation, conflict, and hurt. Things that divide us as people have no power when laughter helps us drop old prejudices and grievances.

Laughter is God's welcoming Spirit at work in a troubled world. This Spirit reminds us that we are part of a whole, living in togetherness rather than isolation. It promotes love, not fear, and hope rather than despair.

Author and Director of *The Happiness Project and Success Intelligence*, Robert Holden, Ph.D., believes so strongly in laughter that he attempted to bottle laughter as a precious commodity. Setting up a special studio, he invited people from all ages and backgrounds to participate in celebrating life with laughter. From nine hours of recorded laughter, he distilled 30 minutes into *The Laughter Album*. Holden states that when you listen to the album, you are reminded of two great truths: 1) laughter is our universal language, and 2) laughter is the best medicine.

According to Holden's philosophy of the universality of laughter, we can use it to build bridges between people regardless of age, gender, race, education, income, and intelligence. Barriers have no strength with shared moments of laughter. Holden also argues that laughter is a basic human need. Because of that, it can function as medicine.

Laughter is gaining bigger acceptance as medicine. Dr. William Fry, an American psychiatrist who has studied the benefits of laughter for the past 30 years, shares his findings on the relationship of laughter, levity, and having a sense of humor with health. Dr. Fry writes in *Psychology Today* that many studies haves shown the links between the ability to laugh daily and the lowering of the stress hormone cortisol. (Cortisol is a stress-induced chemical that can lead to heart disease, high blood pressure, and excess belly fat.)

Because of the medicinal power of laughter, it is part of healing programs for easing pain in hospitals, cancer treatment centers, and pediatric wards. Just like healthy exercise, the act of laughing by releasing endorphins naturally lifts the mood and boosts energy.

Knowing the powerful punch that laughter carries, we cannot dismiss the opportunity for a good laugh. Embracing laughter is good for what ails you.

GOD'S INVITATION: OPTIMISM

Laughter is a way of seeing God at work in the world. But we often must cultivate laughter. It puts a lighter spin on the world that yields **optimism**. Optimism arrives as the outcome of laughter.

Alan Watts, an English philosopher and expert in comparative religions, stated, "The whole art of life is knowing how to transform anxiety into laughter." The transformation starts with facing our fears and the missteps we make. Instead of succumbing to their negativity, we need to laugh at our foibles. Then we can see them as stepping-stones to optimism.

Surrounding ourselves with positive energy provides a platform for optimism. We are the average of the five people that we spend the most time with. So, it's vital that we monitor the incoming energy from others. We need to spend less time with those that bring foulness into our lives through negativity and more time with those who promote laughter.

To discover who adds or drains laughter from your life, try a week of monitoring your energy input or output based on the Energy Monitoring System, or EMS. To initiate this system, you will need a record book. In it, divide two pages into three columns each. On each page, label each column heading as follows: Name, Time, and Feeling.

On this first page, examine your interaction with the five most toxic people in your life—those that suck away your optimism. Consider putting the following people on the list: braggarts, complainers, self-created victims, degraders, abusers, mopers, judgers, uncooperatives, and problem spawners. Here's how to fill in your columns:

- **Name column:** List the names of the top five toxic people in your life. (If you are worried about someone seeing the names, use pseudonyms.)
- **Time column:** Record how much time you spend with the person.
- **Feeling column:** Define the emotions you feel when you are with each person.

For example, I might list Connie's name as a toxic person in my life and then record two hours spent with her on a volunteer project. In the third column, I would define how I feel when I'm with her—exhausted. I don't need to justify why I feel as I do, but rather just take note of how I feel.

On the second page, analyze the five most positive people in your life. These should be ones who support, nourish, and uplift you. Consider those who demonstrate these traits: laughter, compassion, kindness, serenity, attentiveness, cooperation, acceptance, hopefulness, and wisdom. Here's how to address each of the three columns:

- **Name column:** List the names of the people who are positive influences.
- **Time column:** Log in the hours you spend with them.
- **Feeling column:** Define the corresponding emotions you feel when you are around them.

For example, 20 minutes spent chatting over a cup of coffee with Victoria always perks me up. After listing Victoria's name in the first column, I would put our 20 minutes together in the second column. In the third column, I would write down the word "energizing," as her conversation is full of laughter.

At week's end, review your results. Notice correlations between time spent and the how these individuals affect you. Drawing your own conclusions, you may need to set boundaries with some people to reduce the negativity in your life and to increase boundaries with others to create more optimism. We do have the power to enhance our lives with joy and optimism. We can transform our fears and doubts into laughter.

PRAYER

Dear Lord, Let me delight in your world finding the joy in my daily life. Let me laugh my way to heaven for the eternal celebration.

27
CHASING JOY

The purpose of life is to live it, to taste experience to the utmost, to reach out eagerly and without fear for newer and richer experience. —Eleanor Roosevelt

"What do you mean you're leaving?" my friend blared at me. My colleague and boss had multiple reasons to demand a rational answer. Her mouth hung open in disbelief.

As we sat in her office working on next year's budget for the school district, I'd dropped the bombshell—that my husband and I had decided to move.

"You are too young too retire, and you still have so much to give," she cajoled. She pleaded for me to stay the course as she tried to pile on insurmountable reasons against leaving.

Stress shot both our body postures rigid. Shuffling in my seat, I tried to defend my choice. I shared our reasons to pack up our lives and move from California to Montana. My words sounded feeble. I even wondered about the sanity of pulling up stakes to move to a state that we had only visited once before.

Even my sister told me never to tell anyone that I was moving away from Del Mar. "If you tell people, they will surely lock you up!" she barked over and over. "It's moving from Paradise to the back woods."

She did have a point. Del Mar had a perfect blue-sky climate year round. We were headed to Whitefish to battle gray snow-laden clouds and long winters. On top of the weather, I had no idea what I was going to do in Montana. But we were both ready for the next step.

My friend and sister were right. I enjoyed the charmed life that I had worked so hard to attain: a good job and a nice home in a great place to live. I had finally worked my way up the ladder to a dream position at the San Diego County of Education working with close friends to create better schools.

But something deep inside me rumbled. I wondered if my soul was talking to me. While reflecting on why I yearned to move, I realized that a summons sprang from a side of me that I had so often dismissed in order to play it safe, by the rules, and follow the norm. With a growing discontent inside, I came to see my career in education leading me away from my destiny. As a caregiver, I had been drawn to education to help children and teach kids. I yearned to be the kind of teacher that created a fun, non-threatening learning environment where kids could see their own worthiness. That would put them on the right road for life.

As I moved though the ranks from teacher, to principal, to county office coordinator, my career actually took me further and further away from what had drawn me to the teaching profession in the beginning. My calling was to be a teacher in order to help kids, not function as an administrator. Although I still worked for the kids, I no longer worked with them. Balancing budget sheets, developing curricula, and designing administrative programs fed my checkbook better, but failed to feed my soul. The rumbling in my soul grabbed my attention. Discontentment helped me see my career choices as the wrong path. Each step up the educational hierarchy moved me further away from my calling.

I had seen my life's landscape shift before. Twice. Both times, I knew I needed to change, but stalled on hurdling the obstacles to the next step. One happened after six years of service as a nun. Because the next step eluded me, I submitted to a seventh year in the convent and sunk into a year of black depression. The other happened in my 12-year marriage. I stalled on bringing up divorce for so long because I feared the next steps on my own. In both of these circumstances, I tried to squelch the disquieting feelings coming from deep within me. Eventually, they yielded gut-wrenching experiences that forced me to listen to my soul.

This time with my career, I had learned to heed the tug of my heartstrings. I had to depart the public education world to make a change for myself.

I packed up my belongings, said my good byes, and started off to the wilderness of Montana. I heeded the voice of my soul. I left in search of my bliss.

FOLLOWING YOUR BLISS

We've all heard of love at first sight. It's when the heart and soul scream, "Yes, this is the one!" This phenomenon brings feelings of emotional intensity. Partners languish deliriously dizzy from the physical and cosmic attraction. But individuals can also experience the high feeling by themselves. For me, the feeling comes when I find my destiny…when I understand how and why I am on this earth. It's when my whole soul gushes, "Yes, this is why I'm here!"

The recognition of purpose brings sheer contentment, blissful joy, and a relaxed peacefulness. It comes with the strength of conviction that we have chosen the right track, in spite of earthly setbacks. This feeling of being in the right place, at the right time and doing the right thing brings peace to the soul. The restlessness inside subsides.

When we recognize our purpose, we seem to be in syncopation with the universe, effortlessly breathing in and breathing out, gliding through life. We don't have to strain, worry, or stress to make things work. We are in an energetic field of joyful motion knowing that we have found our place and our why. Ours cups overflow, as the Bible says. Our hearts float, and our souls sing. There we find happiness. There we find God.

Once I heard a saying: "If you love what you do, you will never work a day in your life." At the time, the feeling was not a part of my life. Those who achieved that state were lucky, and I wondered what that state would feel like. The aphorism baffled me because each day I dragged myself to work, not recognizing my soul's urge. I enjoyed my work, but my soul did not sing.

After fifty-plus years, I recognized God as my destiny. My calling is to be a spiritual teacher. True joy descends on me when I write, coach, and teach others to empower themselves to find their own bliss. In turn, I feel the love-at-first-sight bliss.

Frequently at book signings or workshops, I meet people who resonate with my messages. They share their struggles or secrets with me. They can't thank me enough for helping them move on with courage. They enjoy the road to living life on their own terms and finding their happiness. I respond with overwhelming gratitude for them.

Yes, it's that feeling of being overwhelmed with gratitude, of being truly blessed to love what I do. Oscar Wilde is right: the two most important days are the day you were born and the day you discover why! Those are days of joy.

GOD'S INVITATION: JOY

What is joy? Joy is the emotion of happiness on steroids. This internal well bubbling over in a stream of happiness springs up to nourish our souls. But grasping joy can be a mystery for some. The good news is that we can attain joy. We don't have to wait for Fed-Ex to deliver a box of happiness to our doorsteps.

In the search for joy and happiness, many people get sidetracked on pursuing success. They work, toil, plan, and sacrifice to get ahead. But happiness is not found in a paycheck or fame.

A truly joyful person has perspective, assimilating the world and its happenings according to the highest good or the bigger plan. When things happen to you, either good or bad, step out of your own perspective to play God. See how everything will work out for the best. Eventually. In God's time, not ours.

We can practice integrating joy into our lives. It's easier than we would think. Sometimes the mere practice of consciously seeking the joy that is already in our lives enhances its presence, for joy tends to breed more joy.

To fulfill our destiny, the monitoring of personal joy is imperative. Creating a **Joy Wheel** is one tool that can help us recognize the joy in our lives. The wheel is comprised of four quadrants:

- Friends
- Family
- Job
- Hobbies/Entertainment/Recreation

You can make your own wheel by folding paper in fourths and titling each quadrant with the above elements. Over a week, document moments of joy found in each of the quadrants. They can be moments of receiving or giving joy. Here's a sample of joys you can include in your wheel:

- **Friends:** Eating lunch out with my best friend. Going on a walk with a friend.
- **Family:** Sharing something at dinner we each enjoyed during our day. Cleaning up after dinner together.
- **Job:** Helping a coworker complete a project. Aiding a customer in solving a problem.
- **Hobbies/Entertainment/Recreation:** Walking outside in the sunshine. Going to yoga class. Reading a book.

Being attentive to feelings of happiness during the day helps to increase our joy. Documenting where and how you find joy in each of the four areas serves as proof for its presence and definitive methods for creating more.

Celebrate happiness spilling over from your Joy Wheel. The daily joy you discover will help you remain faithful to your why, your reason for being on earth and your calling. It will also serve as a wellspring of happiness to share with others.

PRAYER

Dear Lord, let a joyful heart be mine. Show me the way to listen and connect to my true Divine calling.

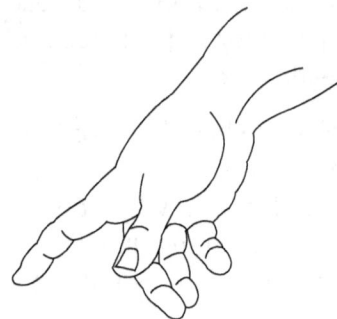

NOTE FROM PATTY

Hope you enjoyed G-vites, giving you practical ways to build your relationship with God. Reviews are the best gift an author can receive. Not only do reviews give us insights on how our message are being received, but they also encourage us. Please take a minute to post a review on the site where you bought this book –it's generally very easy to do. I'd be "eternally grateful".

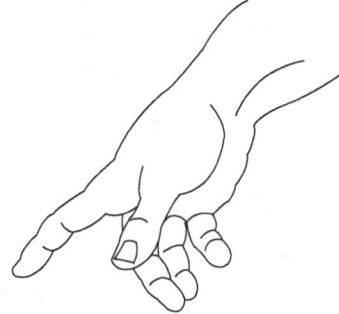

ACKNOWLEDGEMENTS

A book is never just about the author, but the sharing of many gifts and talents of the assembled team. I am blessed and forever grateful to:

- Becky Lomax, editor, writing coach, friend, and cheerleader extraordinaire! This book would never come to be except for Becky's literary skills and personal coaching.

- Callie Spencer for bringing the concept of G-vites to life in the over-the-top graphic design for the cover.

- Sally Hecht for her personal and professional interest, and endless hours of proofreading to provide input to my tunnel vision!

- Phil Wagner for sharing his personal pain and successful strategies for coping with some of life's hardest adversities.

- Loree Bishoff, Barbara Henski, Nancy Mills, Linda McCarthy, and Lisa Colman, my Inner Circle of support, for their unforgettable words of encouragement.

- Patricia Brooks and the Scottsdale Society of Women Writers for their genuine care, encouragement, and the promotion of the works of others.

- Vickie Mullins and her team at Perfect Bound Marketing for their untiring attention, support, and patience in the printing of this beautiful book.

- Alesha Nicole Corey from Above and Beyond Communication for her nonstop promotional efforts.

All my love goes to my husband, **Joe**, who has been there from the first page through the last of two books, far above and beyond the duties of a husband. I finally appreciate his anal retentiveness!

And to my readers, thank you, for your inspiration and reason to share my quest.

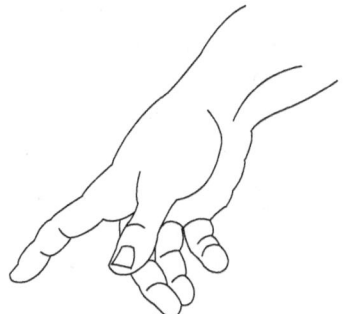

ABOUT PATTY

Patty Ptak Kogutek started her quest to conquer guilt as a Catholic nun. Following seven years in the Servants of Mary Convent in Omaha, Nebraska, she moved to California where she served for twenty-six years in public education as a teacher, school librarian, principal, and school district coordinator. She published her educational policy doctorate on win-win negotiations at the University of Southern California. Since retiring from public education, she self-published her memoir titled *A Change of Habit: A Spiritual Journey From Sister Mary Kateri to Sister Mary Vodka*. She has parlayed her teaching into helping others who wrestle with guilt. She teaches workshops on kicking the habits of guilt, blogs regularly about spirituality, and publishes a daily tip on curing anxiety guilt. Men and women of all faiths have identified with her search for a meaningful relationship with her Creator. Those who started in a traditional organized religion, but found the same emptiness as Patty, glean inspiration from her discovering the God within. Patty donates a percent of profits from her book sales to Servants of Mary Convent, where she served as a nun, and North Valley Hospital in Whitefish, MT where she served as its capital campaign chair. She is an active member of Authors of the Flathead in Montana and Scottsdale Society of Women Writers in Arizona.

LET'S STAY IN TOUCH

Here's my contact information:

Website: www.pattykogutek.com

Weekly Blog: pattykogutek.com/spiritually-speaking

Daily inspiration: pattykogutek.com/inspirational-insights

Twitter: @pattykogutek

Facebook: www.facebook.com/Patty-Kogutek-Author-263832907009510/timeline

Pinterest: www.pinterest.com/pkogutek/

Instagram: instagram.com/pattykogutek_inspiration/

www.ingramcontent.com/pod-product-compliance
Lightning Source LLC
Chambersburg PA
CBHW050534300426
44113CB00012B/2097